Practice of the Love of Jesus Christ

Saint Alphonsus Liguori

A New Translation by Peter Heinegg
With an Introduction by J. Robert Fenili, C.Ss.R.

Liguori

Tercentenary painting of Saint Alphonsus by G. A. Lomuscio

Published by Liguori Publications • Liguori, Missouri
www.liguori.org

The work is translated from the Italian edition published by *Edizione PP. Redentoristi*, Rome, 1953, and entitled *Pratica di Amar Gesu' Cristo.*

Library of Congress Cataloging-in-Publication Data

Liguori, Alfonso Maria de', Saint, 1696–1787.
[Practica di amar Gesu' Cristo. English]
The practice of the love of Jesus Christ / by Saint Alphonsus Liguori: a new translation by Peter Heinegg: with an introduction by J. Robert Fenili.
p. cm.
ISBN 978-0-7648-0031-3
1. Love—Religious aspects—Catholic Church—Early works to 1800. 2. Spiritual life—Catholic Church—Early works to 1800. 3. Catholic Church—Doctrines—Early works to 1800. I. Title.
BV4639.L482513 1997
248.4'82—dc21 96–37868

Liguori Publications, a nonprofit corporation, is an apostolate of the Redemptorists. To learn more about the Redemptorist Congregation, visit *Redemptorists.com.*

Printed in the United States of America
15 16 17 18 19 / 16 15 14 13 12

Contents

Introduction

The Teacher of Prayer

When a saint is declared *Doctor Ecclesiae* in the Catholic Church—a phrase usually translated "Doctor of the Church," although the idea in Latin is "Teacher of the Church"—it is not unusual that a kind of nickname is added based on some particular characteristic of the person or some contribution made to the Church. For Saint Alphonsus Liguori, two nicknames grew up: "The Very Zealous Teacher," because of his unbelievable dedication to his pastoral work, and "The Teacher of Prayer," because of his role in handing on the spirituality of the Catholic Faith.

Born in 1696 near Naples, Italy, he eventually became a successful lawyer, mostly due to the unswerving pressures of his father, Don Giuseppe Liguori, a rich and prominent captain in the royal navy. But just as Alphonsus's career as a young lawyer was beginning to peak, he lost a prestigious case due to behind-the-scenes cronyism and bribery. His youthful idealism, which made him believe in the triumph of honesty and justice in the law system, was so crushed that he fell into a deep depression. His disillusionment was voiced in a phrase which has found its way into every one of his biographies: "O world, now I know what you are like!" After a month of hiding at home, he ventured back to his charitable work as a hospital volunteer. As he was busy with the sick one day, he had a profound religious experience in which he sensed God calling him: "Alphonsus, leave the world and follow me."

Shortly thereafter, he went to a chapel of Our Lady of Mercy and laid on her altar his sword, the official insignia of his status as a nobleman. Then, against the strong objections and maneuvering of his father, he began seminary studies and became a priest.

From his childhood, Alphonsus had been dedicated to prayer. It was something he learned from his mother, Dona Anna Cavalieri. She also imparted to him a tenderness of spirit, which showed its good side in his sensitive and affectionate style of prayer and of dealing with people, but which had its dark side in an overly scrupulous worry about sin. Early in life he began a practice of daily prayer in the presence of the Holy Eucharist. The sense of Christ's presence that he experienced there was so profound that he often lost track of time and his surroundings. We read of a young seminarian who also had this practice of frequent visits to churches and who wanted to meet Alphonsus after he noticed him at such fervent prayer. But the young man finally gave up because Alphonsus took so long in these prayerful visits! (The young man eventually met Alphonsus, became a close friend, and joined him as a member of the Redemptorists.)

Alphonsus quickly gained immense popularity as a preacher and confessor. Even as a seminarian, he had already dedicated himself to the poor underclass of Naples, the people Church leaders did not care about. He began to form these unlettered people into prayer groups led by other laypersons, which met regularly for religious instruction and the practice of meditation. This was the beginning of his path toward being characterized as "The Teacher of Prayer." He had discovered a way to lead any person, regardless of education or occupation, into what today we call a "contemplative attitude," a deep sense of the spiritual side of life. He later found his call to people even more neglected by the Church in the countryside outside the big cities. He founded a group of men (the Congregation of the Most Holy Savior, later changed to the Congregation of the Most Holy Redeemer, who became known as "Redemptorists") to minister to these people by means of itinerant preaching, a kind of regular round of "revivals" that were meant to initiate people into the "Devout Life," a style of daily prayer that would permeate their life with Faith. The more Alphonsus became acquainted with these simple, illiterate people, the more he began to develop a simple, clear style of preaching. He soon began to compose popular hymns and short "meditations" to be read aloud to the people who gathered to spend time in "mental prayer," that is, in quiet meditation as a group. He also began to publish more sophisticated works for those who could read: priests, nuns, and educated laypeople. By the end of his life in 1787, he was among the most widely read spiritual authors in Italy, with his material beginning to appear in other European languages. This "Teacher of Prayer" became one of the most powerful voices in handing on the spirituality of the Catholic Church as it passed through the turmoil of the Age of Enlightenment.

Alphonsus the Writer

I believe one can confidently assert that Alphonsus's writings were the most influential force in shaping the nature of Catholic spirituality of the past two centuries. This force was exerted in two related fields which ultimately were unified in his view: moral theology and devotional prayer. In the field of moral theology, he was named the patron of moral theologians and of confessors, and his moral teachings, though at first suspect and denounced for laxity, became the foundation for moral education in the Church; they also laid the groundwork for the developments in this field that surround the Second Vatican Council.

When we turn to his writings on spirituality, the sheer number of editions they have gone through, together with the extent of translations, indicate the power of his pen. Besides his writings in other areas—they range from a manual on Italian grammar and on mathematics to his classic *Theologia Moralis*—he published seventy-six works on asceticism and spirituality. These went through at least seventy-nine reprints in his own lifetime; his *Visits to the Blessed Sacrament* alone was reprinted thirty-nine times before he died. Countless translations and editions have appeared since his death; the most authoritative listing indicates, for example, that between 1978 and 1988 alone, forty-six translations and editions have appeared in six languages.[1]

Where did this power come from? I would suggest that it arose from several unique characteristics of his spiritual journey. First, there was the particular grace he received from God. In his own life, the practice of prayer was part of his personality from his infancy. So there was an experience of a well-integrated spirituality that was not superadded to his life, but woven into its every step. Alphonsus spoke out of the experience of prayer, not out of theory. And, while this characteristic is also true of other great spiritual leaders and saints, Alphonsus added a further insight into a spirituality for the simple, untutored, uneducated heart. His life was dedicated to bringing a deeper faith to people whose contact with the official Church was minimal and whose lives were beset with superstition, ignorance, and poverty. His life among them fostered in him an ability to lay his finger on what is "child-like" in the human spirit, that inner simplicity where the soul touches the Spirit. His writing is therefore different from that of a spiritual writer whose work is directed primarily toward the educated and sophisticated.

This quality of Alphonsus's spirituality has been described as inviting the person into "sympathetic partnership with God."[2] It is based on the principle that the relationship with God is one of being invited (not forced) into partnership in the ongoing life of the Spirit in the world as formed by human decisions and actions. This is an underlying motif in sections of this work, such as those on the prayer of petition.[3] Alphonsus found this quality to be true of his own life, and he discovered it again when, as a confessor and spiritual director, he began aiding unlettered people in the task of making upright moral decisions. Alphonsus discovered that sin and virtue are not ultimately determined by conformity to law (which presupposes learning and education), but by discerning life's direction in the heart (conscience) of the person. Thus Alphonsus shows prayer to be an essential ingredient in the moral life, and his role as confessor uncovered a profound respect for the dignity of the person which lies at the heart of true spirituality.

Alphonsus holds that the essence of the spiritual life, the "Devout Life," lies in doing the "Will of God"; for him this means opening oneself to the unique, unrepeatable call being directed to the individual.[4] The "Devout Life" promoted by Alphonsus is not a series of servile devotions, or a routine of prayers; it is the shaping of life by grasping Christ's attitude toward us. One reaches this vision by meditation on the mystery of Jesus Christ and discovering for oneself the profound love he has for each of us. And the simplest among us can grasp this.

Thus Alphonsus's spirituality is Christ-centered. It is deeply person-to-person. So it expresses itself as emotional, affectionate, and, in fact, passionate. Prayer for Alphonsus is, first of all, "mental prayer," not vocal or formula prayers. Alphonsus's teaching is a spelling out of Christ's saying: "Where one's treasure is, there is one's heart." We value what we feel strongly about. A person's feelings both grow out of his or her view of life and help to shape that view. There is to be a constant interchange between what we understand and what we feel; and emotions are most deeply tied to our contacts with other persons. Hence the centrality of Christ. He does not teach us about God; he is God loving us. The teaching of God is not by word but by being; "The Word became flesh." So for Alphonsus, our task is to let our flesh become Word. The heart of Alphonsus's prayer lies not in understanding what God has done, but in feeling what God is doing. Hence the passionate tone of Alphonsus's writing.

In contrast to the works of spiritual leaders who addressed the educated, Alphonsus formulated a simple "method" of prayer centered on Christ and available to anyone who has feelings. It centers on five uncluttered steps, so general they cannot be called rules. Their generality stems from Alphonsus's realization that the uniqueness of each person cannot be made to fit into a detailed plan. The first step is to focus one's attention (e.g., through acts of faith in God's presence, humility, sorrow, request for light). Second, one places one's imagination at the service of prayer, primarily by meditating on a text or scene from Scripture, because there are no affections without imagery. Third, one begins to speak out the feelings (affections) that emerge (e.g., thanksgiving, praise, awe, love, insignificance, joy, and so on) and to request what one senses one needs (petition). It is here that Alphonsus locates his role of teaching us how to stimulate and express these "affections." (Alphonsus is not, however, "charismatic," in the sense of evoking emotional responses that manifest unusual external prodigies.) He also models for us the type of petition which flows from these affections. They are not requests for "things," but the outpourings of a deepening desire to sound the depths of love. Fourth, one makes resolutions or decisions; these are the necessary consequences of affirming the value of what we have come to see and feel. These resolutions are a step toward "putting on the Lord Jesus Christ," because they begin to shift the pattern of our lives. Finally, mental prayer is concluded with a short thanksgiving and a request to be faithful.[5]

One characteristic of Alphonsus's writings that may not easily relate to current treatments of spirituality is his distinction between "meditation" and "contemplation." In the present-day language of spirituality, we are asked to try to enter a "contemplative state," a simple "nondiscursive" (quiet, nonverbal) state of experience of God. In Alphonsus's context, contemplation has a different meaning. Alphonsus sees mental prayer as "contemplative" in the sense of focusing on the presence of God, but he does not see in such prayer an effort to be as nondiscursive as some modern approaches seem to suggest.

"Contemplation is very different from meditation. In meditation, God is sought after by a discursive effort; in contemplation there is no effort of this kind as God has been found and is gazed at."[6] This latter step is sheer gift and blossoms unannounced in the course of meditation. To be contemplative is to allow God the opportunity to take over the "conversation." We utterly respect the freedom of God to do so; we cannot manipulate it, we cannot force it; we do not even actively seek it. The opening we offer God lies in actively pouring out our affections and emotions in response to the love we already perceive, trusting we will then be surprised by a new revelation of this love which unites us to God. This method was successful for Alphonsus, for his biographers note the almost constant ability he showed to be lost in the experience of God, as well as the great suffering he endured in the moments when God hid his face.

Another characteristic of Alphonsus's spiritual writing is his wide learning and ability to focus it on the task of prayer. As we read his works, beyond the frequent citations from the Bible, we are constantly finding references to the early *Doctores Ecclesiae*, to the great spiritual writers of the past, and to authors who were popular in the time of Alphonsus. He loved to take a particularly astute or poetic statement from these people (usually quoting the Latin original, as was the custom) and weave it by a paraphrase into the fabric of his writing. In this way, he passed on to his largely illiterate audience the wisdom of the Church. His writings are almost an anthology of the refined experience of centuries of Christian saints and mystics. We should especially notice the number of women from whom Alphonsus draws his inspiration. Without parallel is Saint Teresa of Ávila; Alphonsus treats her like a beloved older sister who seems to appear on almost every other page of his writings. But other women mystics popular in his day (e.g., Saint Mary Magdalen de Pazzi, Venerable Battista Varani, Saint Catherine of Genoa) make frequent appearances as well. The most frequently quoted book of the Hebrew Scriptures in Alphonsus's writings is The Song of Songs; the feminine perspective of this book indelibly marks his writings.

The Practice of the Love of Jesus Christ

This mature work is said to sum up Alphonsus's spirituality and moral teaching into a well-integrated whole. Some of its characteristics are worthy of note. First, the title, which can be simply translated as "How to Love Jesus Christ." This points out a basic characteristic of Alphonsus's spiritual teaching: its practicality. It explains much of the popular appeal his works have enjoyed: here's a "how-to-do-it" book.[7] Like amateur carpenters or cooks or home decorators in their area of interest, all of us want to know "how to do it" when it comes to life. And so Alphonsus set out to write practical manuals on the one hand (e.g., his *Praxis Confessarii [How to Hear Confessions]* for uneducated country clergymen) and, on the other, simple collections of reflections which would invite a person to pray (Alphonsus knew that the only practical way to "teach" someone how to pray is to stimulate the affections).

Furthermore, *The Practice of the Love of Jesus Christ* is a how-to-do-it book written for people who could read. Unlike other works of Alphonsus which were written to be read out loud, this was written to be read in the quiet of one's "upper room." It is a familiar, friendly conversation with someone about a mutual friend named Jesus Christ. But it remains written in Alphonsus's usual straightforward, conversational style; there is no jargon, no attempt to sound "profound."

Also, this book is an extended commentary on Scripture. This point is often missed when we read one of Alphonsus's devotional works because it is not a commentary in today's usual sense, that is, a book pointing out historical context, literary genre, related texts, and so on. Alphonsus insists, for example, when we pick up his meditations on the Passion of Jesus Christ, that his work is no substitute for the Scriptures. So this book is to be used only to help us notice the heart of what is being proclaimed in the Scriptures: love. In their time, Alphonsus's works were a kind of biblical textbook. The practice of the day was to quote Scripture in Latin; the fallout of the Counter-Reformation had made it suspect, if not downright lethal, to use vernacular translations of the Scriptures. So Alphonsus quotes a passage from Scripture, and then immediately paraphrases it in the Italian of his audience. This often causes a certain redundancy in a translation when both the Latin and Italian are translated into English. We must also recall that Alphonsus used the Latin Vulgate version of the Bible; modern translations have sometimes shown the inaccuracy of the translation which Alphonsus was using; in these cases, Alphonsus's interpretation of the text is more a presentation of the general tradition of the Church than a reflection drawn directly from the sacred text as we know it today.

We must also accept that fact that some sections of this book are marked by historical situations which no longer exist. For example, Alphonsus's treatment of frequent reception of the Eucharist is based on the practice of the time that was much more restrictive than today's. Controversies that were lively in his day have faded into different issues, for example, Jansenism, the Enlightenment. These sections must be read judiciously so that the underlying values are not lost in the trappings of history.

While Alphonsus has organized his book around the text from the thirteenth chapter of Paul's First Letter to the Corinthians (13:4–7), the first four chapters form an introduction which must not be overlooked. These chapters lay out the fundamental principles of Alphonsus's spirituality which are then brought to bear on the reading of the Scripture text. Each of these chapters offers us a motive for why we want to meditate on the biblical description of charity; they basically point out that spirituality results from appreciating different facets of God's love:

1. The suffering and death of Jesus is a cry for love
2. The Eucharist is a lover's gift to his beloved
3. The sense of confidence which arises in the heart as a sign of love
4. The force of God's love in freeing us to respond.

The practical nature of this work is then manifested in the thirteen chapters that follow, each one unfolding practical aspects of love as the apostle Paul has listed them. The dependence of this section on the order of Paul's text obscures the logical connection of chapters and the relative importance of the characteristics treated. The "Abstract of Virtues," which forms the concluding chapter, helps to relate these characteristics more clearly. It shows the practical purpose of the whole work: to begin to form these virtues (habits of good action) which Alphonsus sees as the test of whether the love of Christ has been achieved. It also forms a succinct reference for further reflection and prayer.

One last characteristic of this work which cannot be overlooked are the "Prayers of Love and Affection" at the end of each chapter. Their presence follows a customary practice in the devotional literature of the day. One mistake is to try to recite these prayers like Our Fathers or Hail Marys. These prayers, rather, serve two different purposes. First, they are samples of what Alphonsus sees as the turning point of the meditation process (step three mentioned on page xii): moving from intellectual and imaginative considerations to interior change. In these prayers he is modeling for us how to take this step. He is saying, "This is how I do it; watch, and then you try." Second, they are simply the outbursts of love which Alphonsus experienced at the moment. Notice, for example, how the prayer at the end of the chapter on patience (Chapter V) does not even mention patience! These are not calculated prayers "to be said when..." In these prayers, we see in action what this whole book is about "How to Love Jesus Christ."

J. Robert Fenili, CSsR
Denver, Colorado

I

How Much Jesus Christ Deserves Our Love, Because of the Love He Has Shown Us in His Passion

1 • The sanctity and perfection of a soul consists entirely in loving Jesus Christ, our God, our sovereign good, and our Redeemer. Whoever loves me, says Jesus Christ, shall be loved by my Eternal Father: "The Father himself loves you, because you have loved me" (Jn 16:27). Some, says Saint Francis de Sales, argue that perfection consists in an austere life, others in prayer, others in frequenting the sacraments, others in almsgiving. But they deceive themselves: perfection consists in loving God with our whole heart.[1] The apostle Paul wrote: "Above all, clothe yourselves with love, which binds everything together in perfect harmony" (Col 3:14). Love unites and preserves all the virtues that make a person perfect. Hence Saint Augustine said: "Love God, and do whatever you please,"[2] because a soul that loves God is taught by that same love never to do anything to displease God, and to leave nothing undone that may please him.

2 • Doesn't God deserve all our love? He has loved us from all eternity: "I have loved you with an everlasting love" (Jer 31:3). Look, says the Lord, I was the first to love you. You

were not yet in the world; the world itself wasn't even there, and already I loved you. As long as I am God, I loved you; as long as I have loved myself, I have also loved you. So, when other earthly husbands were offered her, Saint Agnes, that holy young virgin, was quite right to reply: "I am engaged to another lover."[3] Go, she said, O lovers of this world, cease to claim my love; my God was the first to love me. He has loved me from all eternity: thus it is right for me to give him all my affections, and to love none but him.

3 • Seeing that humans are drawn by kindness, God willed to use his gifts to win them over to his love. "I led them with cords of human kindness, with bands of love" (Hos 11:4). I wish to draw men and women to love me with those snares by which they are caught, that is, by the snares of love. And those have precisely been God's gifts to human beings. After having given us souls with powers after his own image, with memory, understanding, and will, and bodies furnished with their senses, he created for us heaven and earth, and so many other things, all for the love of us—the skies, the stars, the planets, the seas, the rivers, the springs, the mountains, the plains, metals, fruits, and countless species of animals: and all these creatures were made to serve the human race, so that men and women might love him in gratitude for so many gifts.

"Heaven and earth," Saint Augustine exclaims, "and all things tell me to love you."[4] My Lord, he said, whatever I behold on the earth, or above the earth, it all speaks to me, and exhorts me to love you; because all things tell me that you have made them for the love of me.

When the Abbe Armand Jean Le Bouthillier de Rancé, the Cistercian founder of La Trappe, looked out from his hermitage and surveyed the hills, the fountains, the birds, the flowers, the planets, and the skies, he felt himself inflamed by each of these creatures to love God who had created them for love of him.[5]

4 • Similarly Saint Mary Magdalen de Pazzi, when she held any beautiful flower in her hand, felt herself on fire with love for God; and she would say: "Then God has thought from all eternity of creating this flower for love of me!" Thus that flower became, as it were, a dart of love, which sweetly wounded her, and brought her closer to God.[6]

On the other hand, Saint Teresa of Ávila said that when she looked at trees, springs, brooks, coasts, or meadows, all these beautiful creatures rebuked her for her ingratitude in loving so little the Creator who had made them in order to be loved by her.[7]

In this vein we are further told of a devout hermit who, when walking through the country, imagined that the plants and flowers in his path reproached him for his ingratitude to God; so that as he went along he would strike them with his staff, and say to them: "Oh, be quiet, be quiet; you call me ungrateful; you tell me God has made you out of love for me, and yet I do not love him. But I've already understood you. Be quiet, be quiet; don't scold me anymore."[8]

5 • But God wasn't satisfied with giving us all these beautiful creatures. To win all our love he has gone so far as to give all of himself to us. "For God so loved the world that he gave his only Son" (Jn 3:16).

When the Eternal Father saw that we were all dead and deprived of his grace because of sin, what did he do? Out of his immense love, indeed, as the apostle Paul writes, out of the all too great love he bore us, he sent his beloved Son to make atonement for us; and so to restore to us the life that sin had robbed us of: "Out of the great love with which he loved us even when we were dead through our trespasses, [God] made us alive together with Christ" (Eph 2:4–5). And in giving us his Son—not pardoning his Son, that he might pardon us—he has given us along with him every good thing, his grace, his love, and paradise, since all these goods are surely much less than his Son: "He who did not withhold his own Son but gave him up for all of us, will he not with him also give us everything else?" (Rom 8:32).

6 • And so the Son, too, through the love he bears us, has given himself completely to us: "Who loved me, and gave himself for me" (Gal 2:20). In order to redeem us from everlasting death, and to win back for us God's grace and our lost paradise, he became man, and took on flesh like ours: "And the Word became flesh" (Jn 1:14). Behold, then, a humbled God, who "emptied himself, taking the form of a slave…and being found in human form" (Phil 2:8). Behold, the Lord of the world lowers himself to the point of taking the form of a servant and of subjecting himself to the miseries that all other human beings endure.

7 • But still more amazing is the fact that he could very well have saved us without dying and without suffering. But no, he chose to live in affliction and contempt and to die in bitterness and ignominy, so that he even died on a cross—the dreadful gibbet designed for criminals. "He humbled himself and became obedient to the point of death—even death on a cross" (Phil 2:8). But why, since he could have redeemed us without suffering, should he choose death, and death on a cross? To show us the love he bore us. "Christ loved us and gave himself up for us" (Eph 5:2). He loved us and, because

he loved us, he gave himself up to sorrow and shame and to a death more painful than anyone on earth ever endured.

8 • Hence that great lover of Jesus Christ, Saint Paul, once said: "The love of Christ urges us on" (2 Cor 5:14). The apostle meant that it is not so much the sufferings of Jesus Christ as the love he showed us in enduring them that obliges, and all but constrains, us to love him. Listen to what Saint Francis de Sales says on this text from Corinthians: "Knowing that Jesus Christ, true God, has loved us so that he suffered death, and death on a cross, for us, doesn't that put our hearts in a vise, and make them feel its force, and squeeze love from them, but with a power that, the stronger it is, the more delightful it is."[9] He goes on to say, "Why, then, don't we cast ourselves on Jesus crucified, to die on the cross with him, who has chosen to die for love of us? I will hold him (we should say), and I will never let him go; I will die with him, and will be consumed in the flames of his love. One flame will consume this divine Creator and his wretched creature. Jesus gives himself unreservedly to me, and I give myself unreservedly to him. I will live and die in his loving arms; neither life nor death shall ever separate me from him. O eternal love, my soul longs after you, and chooses you forever. Come, O Holy Spirit, and inflame our hearts with love. Oh, to love! Oh, to die! To die to all other loves, and to live only for the love of Jesus Christ! O Redeemer of our souls, grant that we may eternally sing, Long live Jesus, whom I love. I love Jesus, who lives for ever and ever."[10]

9 • The love of Jesus Christ for his people was so great that it made him desire the moment of his death, so as to show them the affection he had for them. Hence he used to say in his lifetime: "I have a baptism with which to be baptized, and what stress I am under until it is completed!" (Lk 12:50). I have to be baptized in my own blood; and how strongly I feel myself gripped by the desire that the hour of my Passion may come, so that all people may know the love I bear them! That is why John, speaking of the night on which Jesus began his Passion, writes: "Jesus knew that his hour had come to depart from this world and go to the Father. Having loved his own… he loved them to the end" (Jn 13:1). The Redeemer called that hour *his* hour, because the time of his death was the time he had desired; as it was then that he wished to give humankind the ultimate proof of his love, by dying for them upon a cross, consumed by pain.

10 • But what could ever have led a God to die executed upon a cross between two villains—such a disgrace to his divine majesty? "Who did this?" asks Saint Bernard. "It was love," he answers, "careless of its dignity."[11] See how love, when it wants to make itself known, doesn't go looking for what best befits the dignity of the lover, but what will serve best to show itself to the beloved. So Saint Francis of Paola had very good reason to cry out at the sight of a crucifix, "O love, O love, O love!"[12] Likewise, when we look at Jesus on the cross, we should cry out those very same words.

11 • Indeed, if faith had not assured us of it, who could ever believe that a God, all powerful, most happy, and Lord of the universe would have wished to love humanity so much that he seems to have gone out of himself for the love of us humans? We have seen Wisdom itself, that is, the Eternal Word, go mad from overwhelming love for humanity! That was how Saint Laurence Giustiniani spoke of it: "We see Wisdom itself infatuated through excess of love."[13] Saint Mary Magdalen de Pazzi said the same thing: One day, in ecstasy, she took a wooden crucifix into her hands, and cried out: "Yes, my Jesus, you are mad with love. I say that, and I will say it forever: You are mad with love, my Jesus."[14] But no, says Dionysius the Areopagite: "It is not madness, but the usual effect of divine love, which makes him who loves go out of himself, in order to give himself up entirely to the object of his love."[15]

12 • If people would only stop to consider, looking at Jesus on the cross, the love that he has borne each one of them! "With what love," says Saint Francis de Sales, "would we not be set ablaze at the sight of those flames in the Redeemer's breast! And oh, what happiness, to be able to be burned by that same fire with which our God burns for us! What joy, to be bound to God by the chains of love!"[16] Saint Bonaventure called the wounds of Jesus Christ wounds that cut through the most senseless hearts, and which inflame the most frigid souls.[17] How many arrows of love come forth from those wounds, to strike the hardest hearts! What flames issue from the burning heart of Jesus Christ, setting on fire the coldest souls! And how many chains come from that wounded side to bind the most rebellious hearts!

13 • Blessed John of Ávila was so enamored of Jesus Christ that he never failed in any of his sermons to speak of Jesus' love for us. In a treatise on the love that this most loving Redeemer has for human beings, John has expressed such burning feelings that I wish to insert them here because of their extreme beauty. He writes:[18]

14 • "You, O Redeemer, have loved us in such a way, that anyone who reflects upon this love cannot do less than love you; for your love does violence to hearts: as the Apostle says:

'The love of Christ urges us on' (2 Cor 5:14). The source of the love of Jesus Christ for us is his love for God. That is why he said on Holy Thursday: 'That the world may know that I love the Father. Rise, let us be on our way' (Jn 14:31). But where? To die upon the cross for men and women.

15 • "No human mind can understand how hotly this fire burns in the heart of Jesus Christ. Just as he was commanded to suffer death once, if had he been commanded to die a thousand times, he had enough love to suffer every one of them. And if what he suffered for all people had been imposed upon him for the salvation of a single person, he would have done it for each one as he did for all. And as he hung for three hours upon the cross, so, had it been necessary to hang there until the Day of Judgment, he had enough love to do it. So that Jesus Christ loved much more than he suffered.

"O divine love, how much greater were you than you seemed to be; for so many wounds and bruises tell us of a great love, but they do not tell of all its greatness. There was more within than appears without. That was but a drop that sprang forth from the great sea of infinite love.

"This is the greatest sign of love, to lay down one's life for one's friends." But this sign was not enough for Jesus Christ to express his love.

16 • "This is the love that leaves good souls beside themselves, and makes them stand amazed, when it is granted them to know it. It gives rise to a burning sensation in the gut, to the desire for martyrdom, to bliss in pain, to rejoicing, as Saint Lawrence did, over a red-hot grill, to walking on burning coals as if they were roses, to yearning for torments, to rejoicing in what the world dreads, and embracing what it abhors. Saint

Ambrose says that the soul married to Jesus Christ upon the cross thinks nothing is more glorious than to bear the marks of the Crucified.

17 • "But, my lover, how shall I repay this love of yours? Blood deserves to be recompensed with blood. Let me see myself dyed in this blood and nailed to this cross. O holy cross, receive me too upon you. Crown of thorns, grow wider, that I too may put my head in you. Nails, leave those innocent hands of my Lord and pierce my heart with compassion and love. That, says Paul, is why you died, my Jesus: to take possession of the living and the dead, not with punishments, but with love: 'For to this end Christ died and lived again, so that he might be Lord of both the dead and the living' (Rom 14:9).

18 • "Great thief of hearts, the strength of your love has broken even our hard hearts. You inflamed the whole world with your love. Wisest Lord, inebriate our hearts with this wine, burn them with this fire, pierce them with this arrow of your love. This your cross is indeed a crossbow that pierces hearts. Let the whole world know that my heart is stricken. Sweetest love, what have you done? You have come to heal me, and you have wounded me. You have come to teach me, and you have made me like someone mad. O wisest madness, may I never live without you. Lord, everything that I see on the cross invites me to love: the wood, the form, the wounds in your body; and above all, your love invites me to love you and never to forget you."

19 • But to arrive at the perfect love of Jesus Christ, we must take the necessary steps. Here are the steps that Saint Thomas Aquinas teaches us (*Opusculum De dilectione Dei,* §1):

1. Constantly keep in mind God's benefits, both general and particular.
2. Consider the infinite goodness of God, who is forever doing us good, who always loves us and seeks our love.
3. Diligently avoid the slightest thing that might offend him.
4. Renounce all the goods of this world, riches, honors, and sensual pleasures.

The spiritual writer John Tauler says that another great way to acquire perfect love for Jesus Christ is to meditate on his holy Passion.[19]

20 • Who can deny that, of all devotions, devotion to the Passion of Jesus Christ is the most useful, the most tender, the dearest to God, the one that most consoles sinners and most inflames loving souls? Where else do we get so many blessings as from the Passion of Jesus Christ? Where else do we have hope of pardon, strength against temptations, and confidence that we are going to paradise? Whence come so many bright lights of truth, so many loving calls, so many promptings to change our life, so many desires to give ourselves to God, as from the Passion of Jesus Christ? Thus Paul the Apostle was only too right to declare that those who do not love Jesus Christ are excommunicated. "Let anyone be accursed who has no love for the Lord" (1 Cor 16:22).

21 • Saint Bonaventure says there is no devotion more capable of sanctifying a soul than meditation on the Passion of Jesus Christ. For this reason he advises us to meditate every day upon the Passion, if we want to advance in the love of

God.[20] And before him Saint Augustine, as Bernardinus de Bustis relates, said that shedding one tear in memory of the Passion is worth more than fasting on bread and water every week for a year.[21] That is why the saints have always taken up meditation on the sorrows of Jesus Christ: it was by this means that Saint Francis of Assisi became a seraph. One day a gentleman found him weeping and crying out with a loud voice. On being asked why he did so, he answered, "I weep for the sorrows and ignominies of my Lord: and what makes me weep the most is that we, for whom he suffered so much, live in forgetfulness of him." And on saying this he redoubled his tears, so that this man too began to weep. Whenever the saint heard the bleating of a lamb, or saw anything else that reawakened the memory of Jesus' Passion, he immediately fell aweeping. Another time, when he was sick, someone told him that he should have a book of devotion read to him. "My book," he replied, "is Jesus crucified." Hence he did nothing but exhort his brethren to think of the Passion of Jesus Christ at all times.[22]

Giorgio Tiepolo writes: "Anyone who does not fall in love with God by looking at Jesus dead upon the cross will never fall in love."[23]

Prayers of Love and Affection

Eternal Word! You spent thirty-three years in sweat and hardship. You gave your blood and your life for our salvation. In short, you spared nothing to make us love you. Then how can there be people who know this and yet do not love you? O God, I am one of these ingrates. I see the wrong I have done.

O my Jesus, have pity on me. I offer you this ungrateful heart of mine—ungrateful, but repentant. Yes, above every other evil, my dear Redeemer, I repent having despised you. I repent, and I am sorry with all my heart.

My soul, you love a God who is bound like a criminal for you, a God scourged like a slave for you, a God made a mock-king for you, a God, in short, dead upon a cross for you as if he were a scoundrel. Yes, my Savior, my God, I do love you. Always remind me of everything that you suffered for me, so that I may never again forget to love you.

Ropes that bound Jesus, bind me to Jesus; thorns that crowned Jesus, wound me with love for Jesus; nails that pierced Jesus, nail me to the cross of Jesus, that I may live and die united to Jesus.

Blood of Jesus, make me drunk with holy love. Death of Jesus, make me die to every earthly affection. Pierced feet of my Lord, I embrace you; deliver me from hell, which I have deserved.

My Jesus, in hell I could not love you anymore, but I want to love you always. Save me, dearest Savior, hold me close to yourself, that I may never lose you again.

O Mary, refuge of sinners, and mother of my Savior, help a sinner who wishes to love God, and who pleads with you. Help me for the love you bear for Jesus Christ.

II

How Much Jesus Christ Deserves to Be Loved by Us, Because of the Love He Has Shown in Instituting the Most Sacred Sacrament of the Altar

1 • "Jesus knew that his hour had come to depart out of this world to the Father; having loved his own who were in the world, he loved them to the end" (Jn 13:1). Our wisest Savior, knowing that the time had already arrived for leaving this earth, before he went to die for us, wished to leave us the greatest sign of his love that he could give us; and this was precisely the gift of the most sacred sacrament.

Saint Bernardine of Siena says that people remember more vividly and hold more dear the signs of love shown them in death.[1] So when they come to die, friends are accustomed to leave to the persons they have loved in this life some gift, a garment or a ring, in memory of their affection. But you, my Jesus, in leaving this world, what have you left us in memory of your love? Not a garment or a ring, of course, but your body, your blood, your soul, your divinity, your whole self, keeping nothing for yourself. "He gave you all," says Saint John Chrysostom: "He left nothing for himself."[2]

2 • The Council of Trent says that in this gift of the Eucharist Jesus Christ wanted, as it were, to pour out all the riches of his love for us human beings.[3] And the apostle Paul notes that Jesus wanted to give this gift to human beings on the very same night that men were planning his death: "The Lord Jesus on the night when he was betrayed took a loaf of bread, and when he had given thanks, he broke it and said, 'This is my body that is for you. Do this in remembrance of me'" (1 Cor 11:23–24). Saint Bernardine of Siena says that Jesus Christ, before he died, burning with love for us and not content with preparing to give his life, was driven by the excess of his love to do an even greater deed, which was to give his own body for our food.[4]

3 • This sacrament, therefore, was rightly named by Saint Thomas Aquinas "the sacrament of love, the pledge of love."[5] "Sacrament of love," because it was love alone that led Jesus Christ to give us his entire self in it; and "pledge of love," so that if we had ever doubted his love, we would have in this sacrament a pledge of it. It was as if our Redeemer, in leaving us this gift, had said: Souls, if you ever doubted my love, see how I leave you myself in this sacrament: with such a pledge in hand, you can never again doubt that I love you, and love you very much.

But over and above that, Saint Bernard calls this sacrament "the love of loves,"[6] because this gift includes all the other gifts given us by the Lord—creation, redemption, predestination to glory. So the Eucharist is not only a pledge of the love of Jesus Christ, but of the paradise that he wants to give us. "In which," says the Church, "we receive a pledge of future glory."[7] Hence Saint Philip Neri could find no other name for Jesus

Christ in this sacrament save that of "love." And so, when holy Viaticum was brought to him, he was heard to exclaim, "There is my love; give my love to me."[8]

4 • The prophet Isaiah wanted the whole world to see the loving devices that God had found to make people love him.[9] And who could ever have thought—if he himself had not done it—that the Incarnate Word would place himself under the appearances of bread in order to become our food? "Does it not seem madness, says Saint Augustine, to say: 'Eat my flesh; drink my blood'?"[10] When Jesus Christ revealed to his disciples the sacrament that he wished to leave them, some couldn't bring themselves to believe him; and they took leave of him, saying: "How can this man give us his flesh to eat?... This teaching is difficult; who can accept it?" (Jn 6:52,60).

But what men and women could neither think of nor believe the great love of Jesus Christ has thought of and done. Take and eat, he said to his disciples—and through them to us all—before going off to die. Take and eat! But what sort of food will this be, O Savior of the world, that you wish to give us before you die? "Take, eat; this is my body" (Mt 26:26). This isn't earthly food; it is I myself who give myself entirely to you.

5 • And note how longingly Jesus Christ yearns to come to our souls in holy Communion! "I have eagerly desired to eat this passover with you" (Lk 22:15). So he spoke on that night when he instituted this sacrament of love. "I have earnestly desired"—that, as Saint Laurence Giustiniani writes, was how his immense love for us made him speak.[11]

And so that everyone could easily receive him, he chose to leave himself under the appearance of bread. If he had left himself under the appearance of some rare or very costly food, the poor would have been deprived of him. But no, Jesus wanted to place himself under the form of bread, which costs little and can be found everywhere, so that every person in every country can find him and receive him.

6 • So then, to make us eager to receive him in holy Communion, he not only exhorts us to do so with many invitations: "Come, eat of my bread and drink of the wine I have mixed" (Prov 9:5); "Eat, friends, [and] drink," speaking of this heavenly bread and wine (Song 5:1), but he even imposes on us a command: "Take, eat; this is my body" (Mt 26:26). And still more, so that we may go and receive him, he lures us with the promise of paradise: "Those who eat my flesh and drink my blood have eternal life" (Jn 6:54). "The one who eats this bread will live forever" (Jn 6:58).

Moreover, he threatens us with hell and banishment from paradise if we refuse to take Communion. "Unless you eat the flesh of the Son of man and drink his blood, you have no life in you" (Jn 6:53). These invitations, these promises, and these threats all come from the great desire he has to come to us in this sacrament.

7 • But why is it that Jesus Christ so longs for us to receive him in holy Communion? Here is the reason: Dionysius the Areopagite says that love always sighs and aims for union,[12] and we read in Saint Thomas, "Lovers desire to cease being two and to become one."[13] Now this has led the infinite love of God not only to give us himself completely in the eternal kingdom, but even in this life to let men and women possess him in the most intimate union possible, by giving himself to them completely under the appearances of bread in the sacra-

ment. He stands as though behind a wall; and from there he looks at us, as if through a narrow gateway: "Look, there he stands behind our wall, gazing in at the windows, looking through the lattice" (Song 2:9). So we do not see him; but he watches us from there, and is really present there. He is present so that we may possess him, but he hides himself to make us desire him; and until we come to our homeland, Jesus wants to give himself wholly to us, and to remain wholly united with us.

8 • He could not satisfy his love by giving himself entirely to the human race by his Incarnation and by his Passion, dying for all people. He sought to find a way to give himself entirely to each one of us in particular; and so he instituted the sacrament of the altar in order to unite himself fully with each one of us: "Those who eat my flesh and drink my blood abide in me, and I in them" (Jn 6:56). In holy Communion Jesus is united with the soul, and the soul with Jesus; and this is not a union of mere affection, but a true and real union. Hence Saint Francis de Sales says: "In no other action can the Savior be considered more tender or more loving than in this one, where he annihilates himself, so to say, and reduces himself to food, in order to penetrate our souls and to unite himself to the hearts of his faithful."[14] Saint John Chrysostom says that Jesus Christ, through his burning love for us, wished to unite himself to us, so that we might become one and the same thing with him."[15]

9 • "O God, in love with our souls," says Saint Laurence Giustiniani, "you wanted, in a word, to use this sacrament to make your own Heart become a single heart with ours, inseparably united."[16] Saint Bernardine of Siena adds that, "The gift of Jesus Christ to us as our food was the ultimate measure of his love; since he gave himself to us in order to unite himself wholly to us, the way that food becomes one with the eater."[17] Oh, how pleased Jesus Christ is to be one with our souls. One day after Communion he said to his beloved servant, Margaret of Ypres, "See, my daughter, the beautiful union between me and you: come, love me; and let us always remain united in love, and let us never separate again."[18]

10 • So we must be persuaded that a soul can neither do, nor think of doing, anything more gratifying to Jesus Christ than to take Communion with a disposition befitting so great a guest whom we have to receive into our heart. I said "befitting," not "worthy of"; for if we had to have a "worthy" disposition, who could ever go to Communion? Only another God would be worthy to receive a God. By "befitting," I mean the sort of disposition that befits a miserable creature, clothed with the unhappy flesh of Adam.

It is enough that the person, ordinarily speaking, receive Communion in the state of grace and with a strong desire to grow in love for Jesus Christ. "Jesus Christ," said Saint Francis de Sales, "ought to be received solely for love, because he gives himself to us solely out of love."[19]

11 • Next we must realize that there is nothing from which we can reap so great an advantage as from Communion. The Eternal Father has made Jesus Christ the master of all his own divine treasures. "The Father has given all things into his hands" (Jn 13:3). Hence, when Jesus Christ comes to a soul in holy Communion, he brings with him endless treasures of grace. And so after taking Communion one can rightly say: "All good things came to me along with her [wisdom]" (Wis

7:11). Dionysius the Areopagite says that the sacrament of the Eucharist has a supreme power for sanctifying souls, more than all the other spiritual means.[20] And Saint Vincent Ferrer writes that one Communion does the soul more good than a week's fasting on bread and water.[21]

12 • First of all, as the Council of Trent teaches, Communion is the great remedy which frees us from venial, and preserves us from mortal, sins.[22] It says: "We are freed from daily faults" because, according to Saint Thomas, this sacrament stimulates a person to perform acts of love, through which venial sins are forgiven.[23] And Trent says that, "We are preserved from mortal sins," because Communion raises the level of grace, which will save us from serious faults. Hence Innocent III says that Jesus Christ delivered us from the power of sin through his Passion, but that through the Eucharist he delivers us from the power of sinning.[24]

13 • Moreover, this sacrament, above all, inflames our souls with divine love. God *is* love (1 Jn 4:8). And he is a fire that consumes all earthly affection in our hearts. "The Lord your God is a devouring fire" (Deut 4:24). This fire of love is precisely what the Son of God came to ignite on the earth. "I came to cast fire upon the earth," he said, adding that he wanted nothing more than to see this holy fire lit in our souls, "And would that it were already kindled!" (Lk 12:49).

And what flames of divine love Jesus Christ kindles in every person who receives him devoutly in this sacrament! Saint Catherine of Siena once saw the host in a priest's hand take on the appearance of a globe of fire; and the saint was amazed that all human hearts were not burned and reduced to ashes by such a flame.[25] After she took Communion, the face of Saint Rose of Lima shone so brightly as to dazzle those who saw her; and her breath was so hot that a hand held near it felt burned.[26] The story is told of Saint Wenceslaus that merely visiting churches where the Blessed Sacrament was kept inflamed him with such ardor that his servant-companion never felt the cold while walking through the snow if he trod in the footsteps of the saint.[27] Saint John Chrysostom, too, says that the most holy sacrament is a burning fire, so that when we leave the altar we breathe forth flames of love that make us frightening to hell.[28]

14 • The spouse in the Song of Solomon says: "He brought me to the banqueting house, and his intention toward me was love" (Song 2:4). Saint Gregory of Nyssa says that Communion is precisely this banqueting house, where the soul becomes so inebriated with divine love that it forgets itself and loses sight of all created things;[29] and this is the "languishing with love" of which the spouse then speaks: "Sustain me with raisins, refresh me with apples, because I am sick with love" (Song 2:5).

Someone might say: "But this is why I don't go to Communion more often, because I see I am so cold in the love of God." Jean de Gerson answers this sort of person: "So, because you feel cold, you move away from the fire?"[30] Since you feel cold, you should approach this sacrament all the more frequently, so long as you wish to love Jesus Christ. "Even though you feel lukewarm," writes Saint Bonaventure, "approach anyway, trusting in the mercy of God. The sicker you feel, the more you need the doctor."[31] In a similar vein Saint Francis de Sales writes: "Two sorts of persons ought to take frequent Communion: the perfect, in order to stay that way; and the imperfect, in order to reach perfection."[32] But for frequent Communion one must at least have a great desire to become a saint and to grow in love for Jesus Christ. One day the Lord said to Saint

Matilda: "When you go to Communion desire all the love that any heart has ever had for me, and I will receive such a love as you would like it to be."[33]

Prayers of Love and Affection

God of love, O infinite lover, worthy of infinite love, tell me what more can you devise to make us love you? Was it not enough for you to become human, and to subject yourself to all our miseries? Was not it enough for you to shed all your blood for us in torments, and then to die consumed with pain, upon a cross destined for the worst of criminals? Finally, you reduced yourself to hiding beneath the species of bread and wine, to become our food, and so to be joined with each of us. Tell me, I repeat, what more can you devise to make us love you? What wretches we are if we do not love you in this life! When we enter eternity, what remorse will we feel for not having loved you? Jesus, I do not want to die without loving you, and loving you greatly.

I am deeply sorry, and it pains me to have displeased you so often. I repent, and would that I could die of sorrow for it.

But now I love you above all things. I love you more than myself, and I consecrate to you all my affections. May you, who have already given me this desire, also give me the strength to accomplish it.

My Jesus, I desire nothing from you but yourself. Now that you have drawn me to your love, I renounce everything. I cling to you: you alone are enough for me.

O Mary, Mother of God, pray to Jesus for me, and make me a saint. Make this just one more of the many wonders you have done by changing sinners into saints.

III

On the Great Confidence We Must Have in the Love That Jesus Christ Has Shown Us, and in All That He Has Done for Us

1 • David placed all his hope of salvation in his future Redeemer and said: "Into your hand I commit my spirit; you have redeemed me, O LORD, faithful God" (Ps 31:5).

How much more should we put our trust in Jesus Christ, now that he has come and has carried out the work of redemption. Each one of us should say, and keep on repeating with greater confidence: "Into your hand I commit my spirit; you have redeemed me, O LORD, faithful God."

2 • While we have good reason to fear eternal death because of our sins against God, on the other hand we have far greater reason to hope for everlasting life through the merits of Jesus Christ, which count infinitely more for our salvation than our sins count for our damnation. We have sinned and deserved hell; but the Redeemer has come to take upon himself the burden of all our offenses, to make satisfaction for them with his sufferings: "Surely he has borne our infirmities and carried our diseases" (Is 53:4).

3 • At the same unhappy moment in which we sinned, the hand of God had already written down our sentence of eternal death. But what has our merciful Redeemer done? "Erasing the record that stood against us...he set this aside, nailing it to the cross" (Col 2:14). He wiped away with his blood the decree of our condemnation, and then affixed it to the cross, so that when we look at our sentence of damnation for the sins we have committed, we may at the same time see the cross on which Jesus Christ died and blotted it out with his blood, and thus regain hope of pardon and eternal salvation.

4 • Indeed, how much more eloquently does the blood of Jesus Christ speak for us and win mercy for us from God than the blood of Abel spoke against Cain! "[But you have come] to Jesus, the mediator of a new covenant, and to the sprinkled blood that speaks a better word than the blood of Abel" (Heb 12:24). It is as if the apostle Paul had said, "O sinners, how happy you are that, having sinned, you turned to Jesus crucified, who has shed all his blood in order to become the mediator of peace between sinners and God, and to obtain pardon for them. Your iniquities cry out against you, but the blood of the Redeemer pleads in your favor; and divine justice must be appeased by the voice of this blood."

5 • It is true that we shall have to render a strict account of all our sins to the eternal Judge. But who is to be our Judge? "The Father judges no one but has given all judgment to the Son" (Jn 5:22). Let us take comfort, the Eternal Father has given the task of judging us to our own Redeemer; thus Saint Paul encourages us, saying, "Who is to condemn? It is Christ Jesus, who died...who indeed intercedes for us" (Rom 8:34). Who is the judge to condemn us? It is that very same Savior who, rather

than condemn us to everlasting death, was willing to condemn himself and died. And, not content with this, he now continues in heaven to intercede with his Father to gain our salvation. Hence Saint Thomas of Villanova writes: "What do you fear, sinner, if you detest your sin? How will he condemn you, when he died in order not to condemn you? How will he drive you away if you return to his feet, he who came from heaven to seek you out when you were fleeing him?"[1]

6 • And if we are afraid, because of our weakness, of succumbing to the assaults of our enemies, against whom we still must fight, here is what we have to do, as the apostle Paul admonishes us: "Let us run with perseverance the race that is set before us, looking to Jesus the pioneer and perfecter of our faith, who for the sake of joy that was set before him endured the cross, disregarding its shame, and has taken his seat at the right hand of the throne of God" (Heb 12:1–2). Let us go forth to battle with great courage, keeping our eyes on Jesus crucified, who from his cross offers us his help, the victory, and the crown. In the past we fell into sin because we lost sight of the wounds and shame endured by our Redeemer, and so we did not turn to him for help. But if in the future we set before our eyes all he has suffered for love of us, and how he stands ready to help us if only we have recourse to him, we shall certainly not be conquered by our enemies. In her generosity of spirit, Saint Teresa of Ávila used to say, "I cannot understand some people who cry out in terror, 'The devil, the devil!' when we can say, 'God, God!' and make Satan tremble."[2] On the other hand, the saint tells us that if we do not put all our trust in God, all our own exertions will be worth little or nothing. "All our efforts," these are her own words, "are of little use unless we abandon all trust in ourselves and put it in God."[3]

7 • Indeed, what two great mysteries of hope and love we have in the Passion of Jesus Christ and the sacrament of the altar! Who could ever believe these mysteries if faith had not assured us of them? That God almighty should wish to become human, shed all his blood and die in pain upon a cross, and for what? To pay for our sins and save us, rebellious worms! And then his very own body, once sacrificed upon the cross for us, this he is willing to give us for our food in order to make himself one with us! Dear God, these two mysteries should inflame with love and reduce to ashes the hearts of us all. And what sinners are there, be they ever so dissolute, who could despair of pardon if they repent of the evil they have done, when they see a God so in love with human beings and so inclined to do them good? Hence Saint Bonaventure said, "I will have great confidence, in the unshakable hope that he who has done and suffered so much for my salvation will deny me nothing I need."[4]

8 • "Let us, therefore," says the apostle, "approach the throne of grace with boldness, so that we may receive mercy and find grace to help in time of need" (Heb 4:16). The throne of grace is the cross on which Jesus sits, as if on his royal throne, to dispense graces and mercies to all who come before him. But we must quickly turn to him, now that we can find the help we need for our salvation; for perhaps a time will come when we shall no longer be able to find it. Let us go quickly then and embrace the cross of Jesus Christ, and let us go with great confidence. Let us not be dismayed by our miseries; in Jesus crucified we shall find for ourselves all riches and all grace: "For in every way you have been enriched in him...so that you are not lacking in any spiritual gift" (1 Cor 1:5,7). The merits of Jesus Christ have enriched us with all of God's treasures, and have made us capable of every grace that we desire.

9 • Saint Leo the Great says that, "With his death Jesus did us more good than the devil did us harm by sin."[5] And thus he explains what Saint Paul said before him, that the gift of redemption is greater than sin: grace has overcome the offense. "But the free gift is not like the trespass;...where sin increased, grace abounded all the more" (Rom 5:15,20). Hence the Savior encouraged us to hope for every grace and favor from his merits. And see how he teaches us the way to get what we want from his Eternal Father: "Very truly, I tell you, if you ask anything of the Father in my name, he will give it to you" (Jn 16:23). Whatever you desire, he says, ask the Father for it in my name, and I promise you that you will be heard. How could the Father deny us any grace, when he has given us his only-begotten Son, whom he loves as much as himself? "He who...gave him up for all of us, will he not with him also give us everything else?" (Rom 8:32). The apostle Paul says "everything"; no grace is excepted, neither pardon, nor perseverance, nor holy love, nor perfection, nor paradise, "everything else" he has given us. But we must pray to him. God is all generosity to those who pray to him: "[He] is generous to all who call on him" (Rom 10:12).

10 • Here I wish to add some beautiful sentiments from the Venerable John of Ávila, which he has left us in his letters,[6] on the great confidence we should have in the merits of Jesus Christ:

11 • "Don't forget that the mediator between the Eternal Father and ourselves is Jesus Christ, by whom we are loved and clasped by such strong bonds of love that nothing can loosen them, so long as a person does not break them himself by some mortal sin. The blood of Jesus cries out, begging mercy for us, and drowns out the sound of our sins. The death of Jesus Christ has been the death of our sins: 'O Death...where is your destruction' (Hos 13:14). Those who are lost are not lost because they have no means of satisfaction, but because they would not avail themselves, through the sacraments, of the satisfaction given by Jesus Christ.

12 • "Jesus has taken upon himself the task of remedying our ills, as if they had been his own. Thus he has called our sins his own, although he did not commit them, and has sought forgiveness for them. And with passionate love he has prayed, as if he were praying for himself, that all who wish to approach him might be loved. And, as he sought all this, so he gained it, because God has seen to it that Jesus and ourselves are so united that he and we have to be either loved together or hated together. And since Jesus is not and cannot be hated, if we are united with Jesus in love, we too are loved. Since he is loved by God, we too are loved, seeing that Jesus Christ can do more to make us loved than we can do to make ourselves hated; because the Eternal Father loves the Son more than he hates sinners.

13 • "Jesus said to his Father: 'Father, I desire that those also, whom you have given me, may be with me where I am' (Jn 17:24). The greater love conquered the lesser hatred; and thus we have been pardoned and loved. We are sure that we shall never be abandoned where the ties of love that bind us are so strong. The Lord says through Isaiah: 'Can a woman forget her nursing child, or show no compassion for the child of her womb? Even these may forget, yet I will not forget you. See, I have inscribed you on the palms of my hands' (Is 49:15–16). He has graven us on his hands with his own blood. Thus we should not trouble ourselves about anything, since all things have been ordered by those hands that were nailed to the cross in witness of the love he bears us.

14 • "Nothing can so terrify us," continues John of Ávila, "as much as Jesus Christ can reassure us. Let my sins surround me, let my fears of the future accuse me, let the demons lay their snares for me. As long as I beg mercy of Jesus Christ, who is all kindness, who has loved me even until death, I cannot lose confidence; for I see myself so highly prized that a God gave himself for me.

"My Jesus, safe haven for those who seek you out in the storm; my vigilant shepherd, those who do not trust you are deceiving themselves, if only they have the will to amend their lives. That is why you said: Here I am, don't be afraid: I am he who troubles and who consoles. Sometimes I put persons in scenes of desolation that seem like hell; but then I pull them out and console them. I am your advocate; I have made your cause my own. I am your guarantor; I have come to pay your debts. I am your Lord, who redeemed you with my blood, not to abandon you, but to enrich you, having ransomed you at a great price. How shall I flee from those who seek me, when I went forth to meet those who sought to outrage me? I did not turn away my face from those who struck me; and shall I turn it from those who would adore me? How can my children doubt that I love them, seeing me in the hands of my enemies out of love for them? Whom have I ever despised that loved me? Whom have I ever abandoned that sought my help? I go out in search even of those who do not seek me.

15 • "If you believe," concludes John of Ávila, "that the Eternal Father has given you his Son, believe also that he will give you all the rest, which is far less than his Son. Do not think that Jesus Christ is forgetful of you, since he has left you, in memory of his love, the greatest pledge that ever existed—which is himself in the sacrament of the altar."

Prayers of Love and Affection

My Jesus, my joy, what splendid hopes your Passion gives me! How can I be afraid of not receiving pardon for my sins, paradise, and all other graces that I need from an almighty God who has given me all his blood? I know, my Jesus, my hope and my love, that you were willing to lose your life, so I would not be lost.

I love you above everything, my Redeemer and my God. You gave yourself to me completely; I give you all my will, and with it I repeat over and over that I love you; and I wish to keep on saying that I love you. That is what I always want to say in this life and that is how I want to die, breathing my last with these dear words on my lips: My God, I love you; from that moment may I begin a constant love of you that will last to all eternity, and so I will never cease loving you.

Yes, my Jesus, because I love you, I regret more than anything else that I have offended you. Wretch that I am, rather than lose some passing gratification, I have been willing to lose you so often, my infinite good! This thought torments me more than any punishment, but it consoles me to think that

I am dealing with infinite goodness, which will not despise a truly loving heart. My wish is that I could die for you, you who have died for me!

My dear Redeemer, I surely hope from you eternal salvation in the life to come; in this life I hope for holy perseverance in your love; and therefore I intend to keep asking it of you. Through the merits of your death, give me perseverance in praying to you. This, too, I ask and hope of you, O Mary my queen!

IV

How Much We Are Obliged to Love Jesus Christ

1 • As God, Jesus Christ has in himself the right to all our love. But with the love he has shown us, he wished to put us, so to speak, under the necessity of loving him, at least out of gratitude for all he has done and suffered for us. He has greatly loved us that we might love him greatly. "Why does God love, but that he may be loved?" wrote Saint Bernard.[1] Moses had said the same thing long before: "So now, O Israel, what does the LORD your God require of you? Only to fear the LORD your God...[and] to love him" (Deut 10:12). And so the first command that he gave us was: "You shall love the LORD your God with all your heart" (Deut 6:5).

2 • Saint Paul says that love is the fulfillment of the law (Rom 13:10). For "fulfillment" the Greek text has the "completion" of the law. The completion of the law is love. But who, upon seeing a crucified God dying for our love, could resist loving him? Those thorns cry out too loudly, those nails, that cross, those wounds, and that blood, all seeking to make us love him who has loved us so much. One heart is too little with which to love this God who is so in love with us. To match the love of Jesus Christ would take another God to die for his love. "Ah, why," exclaims Saint Francis de Sales, "do we not throw ourselves on Jesus Christ, to die on the cross with him who was pleased to die there for love of us"?[2] The apostle Paul makes it clear that Jesus Christ died for us with this in mind, that we might no longer live for ourselves, but only for the God who died for us: "And he died for all, so that those who live might live no longer for themselves, but for him who died and was raised for their sake" (2 Cor 5:15).

3 • Here the advice of Ecclesiasticus is to the point: "Do not forget all the kindness of your guarantor, for he has given his life for you" (Sir 29:15). Be not unmindful of him who has stood surety for you, who, to atone for your sins, was willing to pay with his death the penalty owed by you.

You should remember how it pleases Jesus Christ that we should frequently recall his Passion. And how it saddens him to see that we ignore it. If a person were to suffer insults, beatings, and imprisonment for one of his friends, how distressed he would be to know that his friend remembered nothing of it and did not even want to hear people talk about it. On the other hand, how gratified would he be to know that his friend always spoke tenderly about it, and often thanked him for it. Thus Jesus Christ is greatly pleased when we recall with loving gratitude his pains and the sorrows and death that he suffered for us.

Jesus Christ was the desire of all the ancients; he was the desire of all the nations before he had yet come to this earth. Now how much more ought he to be our only desire and our only love, now that we see that he has already come, and know how much he has done and suffered for us, even dying upon the cross for love of us?

4 • That was the reason why he instituted the sacrament of the Eucharist on the day before his death, and urged us that as often as we were fed with his most sacred flesh, we should remember his death: "This is my body that is for you. Do this in remembrance of me....For as often as you eat this bread and drink the cup, you proclaim the Lord's death until he comes" (1 Cor 11: 24,26). That is why the holy Church prays: "O God, who in this wondrous sacrament has left us a memorial of your Passion...." And she also sings: "O sacred banquet, in which Christ is consumed, the memory of his Passion is recalled...."[3] So we can understand how pleased Jesus Christ is by those who often think of his Passion, since it was for that very reason that he left himself as a sacrament upon the altar, so that we might have a continuous and grateful recollection of what he suffered for us, and thus our love for him would always increase. Saint Francis de Sales called Mount Calvary "the mountain of lovers."[4] It is impossible to remember that mountain without loving Jesus Christ, who willingly died there for love of us.

5 • O God, why is it that men and women do not love this God who has done so much to be loved by them? Before the Incarnation of the Word, humankind might have doubted whether God truly loved them; but after the coming of the Son of God, and after he died for the love of the human race, how can we possibly go on doubting? "O people of God," says Saint Thomas of Villanova, "look on that cross, on those torments, and on that bitter death, which Jesus Christ has suffered for you: After so many great signs of his love, you can no longer doubt that he loves you very much."[5] And Saint Bernard says that, "The cross and every wound of our Blessed Redeemer cry aloud to make us understand the love he bears us."[6]

6 • In this grand mystery of our redemption, we must consider all the thought and care that Jesus took to discover so many different ways of making himself loved by us. Had he wished to die for our salvation, he need only have died with the other children slain by Herod. But no, he wished before dying to spend thirty-three years in a life full of hardship and pain. And during that life, to win our love he chose to appear to us in different guises. First of all, as a poor baby in a stable; then as a boy-apprentice in a workshop; and finally, as a criminal executed on a cross.

But before dying on the cross, he wished to take on many different heart-wrenching appearances, all to make himself loved: in the agony in the garden, bathed in a bloody sweat; later in the praetorium of Pilate, torn with scourges; then treated as a make-believe king with a reed in his hand, a purple rag on his shoulders, and a crown of thorns on his head; from there dragged through the crowded streets to death, with the cross upon his shoulders; and at last, on the hill of Calvary, hanging on the cross by three iron nails. Tell me, does he or does he not deserve to be loved by us, this God who deigned to suffer so many torments and to use so many ways to capture our love? Father Jean Rigoleu used to say: "I would do nothing but weep for love of a God whose love led him to die for the salvation of his people."[7]

7 • "Love is a great thing," says Saint Bernard.[8] Love is a great and precious thing. Speaking of the divine wisdom, which is holy love, Solomon called it an infinite treasure; because those who have love have become sharers in the friendship of God: "For it is an unfailing treasure for mortals; those who get it obtain friendship with God" (Wis 7:14).

Saint Thomas Aquinas says that love is not only the queen

of all virtues, but that, wherever she reigns, she brings along with her, as if in her train, all the other virtues, and directs them all so that we may be united more closely with God.[9] But properly speaking, it is love that unites us with God, as Saint Bernard tells us.[10]

Scripture tells us many times that God loves whoever loves him: "I love those who love me" (Prov 8:17). "Those who love me will be loved by my Father...and we will come to them and make our home with them" (Jn 14:21,23). "Those who abide in love abide in God, and God abides in them" (1 Jn 4:16). Look at the beautiful union that love creates; it joins the soul to God. Moreover, love gives us the strength to do and to suffer all great things for God: "For love is strong as death" (Song 8:6). Saint Augustine writes: "There is nothing so hard that cannot be overcome by the ardor of love."[11] Because, the saint says, where we love, either we don't feel the weariness, or if we do, we love it."[12]

8 • Listen to Saint John Chrysostom on the subject of what divine love does in the souls where it reigns: "When the love of God has taken possession of a soul, it produces an insatiable desire to labor for the beloved. So much so that however many and great the works that the soul does, and however much time the soul spends in the service of love, it all seems as nothing in its eyes, and the soul is afflicted at doing so little for God; and were it permitted to die and destroy itself for God, the soul would be happy to do so. That is why the soul considers itself useless in all that it does; because as love teaches the soul to know what God deserves, in that clear light the soul sees all the defects of its actions, and derives confusion and pain from them, knowing that its toils for so great a Lord are lowly indeed."[13]

9 • "How indeed those persons delude themselves," says Saint Francis de Sales, "who locate holiness anywhere but in loving God! Some," he writes, "see perfection in austerities, others in almsgiving, others in prayer, others in frequenting the sacraments. For my part, I know of no other perfection than that of loving God with all the heart, because without love all the other virtues are nothing but a pile of stones. And if we do not perfectly enjoy this holy love, the fault lies with us, because we do not end up giving ourselves wholly to God."[14]

10 • One day our Lord said to Saint Teresa, "Everything that does not give me pleasure is vanity."[15] Would that everyone understood this great truth! "There is need of only one thing" (Lk 10:42). It is not necessary to be rich in this world, or to win the esteem of others, to lead a comfortable life, to enjoy honors or a reputation for learning. The one thing necessary is to love God and do his will. This is the only purpose he created us for, this is why he keeps us alive; and this is the only way can we gain admittance to paradise.

"Set me as a seal upon your heart, as a seal upon your arm" (Song 8:6). That is how the Lord speaks to all the souls wedded to him: Set me as a seal upon your heart and upon your arm, so that you may direct to me all your desires and actions; upon your heart, that no other love but mine may enter there, upon your arm so that everything you do may have no other goal but me. Oh, how swiftly people race to perfection when in all their actions they have regard for nothing but Jesus crucified and seek nothing but to give him pleasure!

11 • This, then, should be our only care, to acquire a true love for Jesus Christ. The spiritual masters describe the signs of true love. Love, say they, is *fearful*; it fears displeasing God. It is *generous*, because, trusting in God, it is never dismayed from undertaking even the greatest tasks for his glory. It is *strong*, because it conquers all its evil appetites, even amid the most violent temptations and the darkest desolation. It is *obedient*, because it immediately seeks to carry out God's commands. It is *pure*, because it loves God alone, and only because he deserves to be loved. It is *ardent*, because it would inflame all people and see them consumed with divine love. It is *inebriating*, for it makes the soul live as if it were beside itself, as if it no longer saw or felt or had any senses left for things of this world, and was wholly intent on loving God. It is *unifying*, for it tightly binds together the will of the creature and the will of the Creator. It is *yearning*, for it fills the soul with desire to leave this world, to fly to a perfect union with God in its happy homeland, so as to love him there with all its strength.

12 • But no one teaches the characteristics and true practice of love better than the great preacher of love, Saint Paul. In his First Letter to the Corinthians, he says, first of all, that without love we are nothing, and that nothing is of any use to those without love: "And if I have prophetic powers, and understand all mysteries and all knowledge, and if I have all faith, so as to remove mountains, but do not have love, I am nothing. If I give away all my possessions, and if I hand over my body so that I may boast, but do not have love, I gain nothing" (13:2–3). So if a person had faith strong enough to move mountains, like Saint Gregory Thaumaturgus, the Wonderworker, but had not love, it would do him no good. Were he to distribute all his goods to the poor, and even gladly suffer martyrdom, without love, so that he did it for any other goal than that of pleasing God, it would be of no use to him.

Then Saint Paul points to the signs of true love, and at the same time teaches us the practice of the virtues that are the daughters of love: "Love is patient; love is kind; love is not envious or boastful or arrogant or rude. It does not insist on its own way; it is not irritable or resentful; it does not rejoice in wrongdoing, but rejoices in the truth. It bears all things, believes all things, hopes all things, endures all things" (1 Cor 13:4–7).

Let us, then, proceed in this book to consider these holy practices, to see whether the love that we owe Jesus Christ truly reigns within us, and likewise to learn which virtues we should chiefly train ourselves in, so as to preserve and increase in us this holy love.

Prayers of Love and Affection

O most lovable and loving Heart of Jesus, wretched is the heart that does not love you! O God, you died on the cross, abandoned and wholly bereft, for the love of your people. How then can we live so forgetful of you? O love of God! O human ingratitude! O you of short memory, look upon the innocent Lamb of God, agonizing on the cross and dying for you, in order to satisfy divine justice for your sins, and so draw you to his love. Look how at the same time he prays to his Eternal Father to forgive you. Look at him and love him.

My Jesus, how few are those who love you! Wretch that I am, I, too, have lived for many years unmindful of you, and thereby greatly offended you. My beloved Redeemer, it is not so much the punishment I have deserved that makes me weep, as the love that you have borne me.

May the sorrows of Jesus, the ignominies of Jesus, the wounds of Jesus, the death of Jesus, the love of Jesus thrust themselves into my heart, and may their sweet memory remain there forever to wound me continually and inflame me with love.

I love you, my Jesus; I love you, my sovereign good; I love you, my love, more then my entire being: I love you, and I want that love for you to last forever.

Never let me leave you or lose you again.

Make me completely yours; do it through the merits of your death. In this I firmly trust.

And I have great confidence, too, in your intercession, O Mary, my Queen; make me love Jesus Christ and make me also love you, my mother and my hope!

V

"Love Is Patient": The Soul That Loves Jesus Christ Loves Suffering

1 • This earth is a place for winning merit, and therefore it is a place for suffering. Our true homeland, where God has prepared a place of rest for us in everlasting bliss, is paradise. In this world we have little time to stay, but in that little time we have many travails to suffer: "A mortal, born of woman, few of days and full of trouble" (Job 14:1). There must be suffering, and all must suffer; be they just or be they sinners, each one has a cross to bear. Those who bear it with patience are saved, those who bear it with impatience are lost. Saint Augustine says that the same miseries send some to heaven and others to hell.[1] The test of suffering, he says, separates the wheat from the chaff in the Church of God: those who in times of tribulation humble and resign themselves to the will of God are wheat for paradise; those who grow haughty and enraged, and so forsake God, are chaff for hell.[2]

2 • On the day when the cause of our salvation will be judged, our life must be found to conform to the life of Jesus Christ, if we are to receive the blessed verdict of the predestined: "For those whom he foreknew he also predestined to be conformed to the image of his Son" (Rom 8:29). This was the purpose for which the Eternal Word descended to earth, to teach us, by his example, to carry with patience the crosses that God sends us: "Christ also suffered for you," Saint Peter writes, "leaving you an example, so that you should follow in his steps" (1 Pet 2:21). Jesus Christ chose to suffer so as to encourage us to suffer.

O God, what sort of life did Jesus Christ have! A life of ignominy and pain. The prophet calls our Redeemer "despised and rejected by others; a man of suffering and acquainted with infirmity" (Is 53:3). He was a man despised and treated as the lowest, the vilest of men, yes, a man of sorrows; for the life of Jesus Christ was full of hardships and sorrow.

3 • Now, just as God has treated his beloved Son, so he treats everyone whom he loves, and those whom he takes for his sons and daughters: "For the Lord disciplines those whom he loves, and chastises every child whom he accepts" (Heb 12:6). That is why he said to Saint Teresa one day: "Know that the souls dearest to my Father are those afflicted with the greatest sufferings."[3] Hence the saint, when she found herself in distress, said that she would not exchange her troubles for all the treasures in the world.[4] After her death she appeared to a person, and revealed to her that she was enjoying a great reward in heaven, not so much for her good works, as for the sufferings that she gladly bore in this life for the love of God. She said that if she could possibly desire to return to earth, the only reason would be to suffer some more for God.[5]

4 • Those who love God by suffering earn a double profit in paradise. Saint Vincent de Paul used to say that not to suffer in this life should be considered a great misfortune. And he added that a congregation or individual that does not suffer and is applauded by everyone is not far from a fall.[6] And so if a day went by in which he suffered nothing for God, Saint Francis of Assisi would begin to worry that God had forgotten him.[7] Saint John Chrysostom writes that when God endows anyone with the grace of suffering, he gives that person a greater grace than the power of raising the dead to life; because in doing miracles a person remains God's debtor, whereas in suffering God makes himself the debtor of humankind. And Saint Francis adds that whosoever endures something for God, even if they had no other gift than the strength to suffer for the God whom they love, this would be a great mercy. Thus Chrysostom said he rated higher the grace Paul got from being bound in chains for Jesus Christ than in his being swept up to the third heaven (2 Cor 12:2–4).[8]

5 • "Let endurance have its full effect" (Jas 1:4). This means that nothing is more pleasing to God than to see a soul suffering with patience and peace all the crosses that he sends. Love makes the lover resemble the beloved. Saint Francis de Sales said: "All the wounds of the Redeemer are so many mouths that teach us how one must suffer for him. This is the science of the saints, to suffer constantly for Jesus; and in that way we too shall quickly become saints."[9] A person who loves Jesus Christ wants to be treated like Jesus Christ—treated as poor, tormented, and despised.

Saint John saw all the saints "robed in white, with palm branches in their hands" (Rev 7:9). The palm is the emblem of martyrs, but not all the saints suffered martyrdom. Why, then, do all the saints bear palms in their hands? Saint Gregory replies that all the saints were martyrs either of the sword or of patience. And thus he adds, "We can be martyrs without the sword, if we remain patient."[10]

6 • The merit of a soul that loves Jesus Christ comes from loving and suffering. Here is what the Lord said to Saint Teresa: "My daughter, do you think that that merit consists in enjoyment? No, it consists in suffering and in loving. Look at my life, so full of affliction. Be sure, daughter, that the more my Father loves anyone, the more distress he sends to that person; it is a measure of his love. Look at these wounds, your sufferings will never match them."[11] "It is a great mistake to think that my Father welcomes as friends those who are strangers to suffering."[12] And Saint Teresa adds for our consolation: "God never sends a trial without immediately compensating for it by some favor."[13]

One day Jesus Christ appeared to the Blessed Battista Varani, and told her of three great favors that he does for his beloved souls: the first enables them not to sin; the second, still greater, is to do good works; the third, and the greatest of all, is to suffer for his love.[14] Saint Teresa used to say that whenever anyone does something for God, the Lord repays him or her with some affliction.[15] And therefore when they suffered any trouble, the saints thanked God for it. Speaking of his bondage in Turkey, Saint Louis of France said: "I rejoice, and thank God more for the patience he gave me in the time of my imprisonment than if I had acquired all the earth."[16] And when, after her husband's death, Saint Elizabeth, princess of Thuringia was banished from the country along with her son, and found herself homeless and abandoned by everyone, she went to a Franciscan monastery, and there she had a *Te Deum* sung in thanks to God for favoring her by making her suffer for love of him.[17]

7 • Saint Joseph Calasanctius used to say, "To gain heaven all toils are trivial."[18] And the apostle Paul said it before him: "I consider that the sufferings of this present time are not worth comparing with the glory that is to be revealed to us" (Rom 8:18). It would be much to our advantage to endure all the pains suffered by all the martyrs throughout our lives, to enjoy one single moment of paradise. How much more, then, should we embrace our crosses, since we know that the sufferings of our short life will win us eternal bliss? "For this slight momentary affliction is preparing for us an eternal weight of glory beyond all measure" (2 Cor 4:17).

Saint Agapitus, while only a youngster, replied when he was threatened with death: "And what better fortune could I have than to lose my head here, only to have it crowned in paradise?"[19] This made Saint Francis exclaim: "So very great / is the good I await, / that every pain / strikes me as gain."[20]

But whoever wants the crown of paradise must do combat and suffer: "If we endure, we will also reign with him" (2 Tim 2:12). There is no reward without merit, no merit without patience: "In the case of an athlete, no one is crowned without competing according to the rules" (2 Tim 2:5). And those who struggle with the most patience will have the greatest crown.

How amazing: when it comes to the temporal goods of this earth, worldly people try to get as many as they can; but when it comes to eternal goods, they say, "A little corner in heaven will do." That is not what the saints say: in this life they are content with whatever they get. Yet more, they strip themselves of those earthly goods; but as for the eternal goods, they seek to procure as many as possible. I wonder, which of the two groups is acting more wisely and prudently?

8 • But even speaking of this life, it is certain that those who suffer with more patience enjoy the greater peace. Saint Philip Neri used to say that in this world there is no purgatory; there is either paradise or hell: those who patiently endure tribulations enjoy paradise; those who do not, suffer hell.[21] For, as Saint Teresa writes, she who embraces the crosses sent her by God does not feel them.[22] Finding himself at one point surrounded by all sorts of tribulation, Saint Francis de Sales said, "For some time now all the hostility and secret resistance that have come my way have afforded me a sweet and matchless peace; and they give me the premonition that my soul will soon be anchored in God, which I can say quite truthfully is the only ambition and desire of my heart."[23]

Peace can never be found by anyone who leads a disorderly life, but only by those who live in union with God and with his holy will. A certain missionary, a religious, while in the Indies happened one day to see a condemned man on the scaffold about to be executed. The man called him over and said, "You must know, Father, that I was once a member of your order. So long as I observed the rules, I led a life of perfect contentment; but then when I began to slacken, I suddenly began to find everything difficult; so much so, that I left the religious life, and gave myself up to vices, which have finally brought me to the unhappy end in which you now see me." And, last of all, he said: "I have told you this that my example may be useful to others." The Venerable Father L. da Ponte said, "Take the sweet things of this life for bitter, and the bitter for sweet; and then you will always enjoy peace."[24] Yes, for though sweet things please the senses, they leave behind a bitter taste of remorse in exchange for the flawed satisfaction that most of them provide. But the bitter, when accepted with patience from the hand of God, become sweet and dear to the souls who love him.

9 • Let us be persuaded that in this vale of tears true peace of heart cannot be found except by those who endure and lovingly embrace their sufferings to please God. This is what comes of the state of corruption that has left us all infected by sin. The condition of the saints on earth is to suffer as they love; the condition of the saints in heaven is to enjoy as they love. Father Paul Segneri the younger once wrote to one of his penitents to encourage her in her suffering. He advised her to have these words inscribed at the base of her crucifix: "That is how one loves."[25]

Not just suffering but the will to suffer for the love of Jesus Christ is the surest sign that a soul loves him. "And what greater gain," said Saint Teresa, "can there be than to have some proof that we are pleasing to almighty God?"[26] Alas, the majority of people are dismayed at the mere mention of the cross, of humiliation and pain. Still there are not a few loving souls who find all their happiness in suffering, and who would be almost inconsolable were they to pass their time on earth without suffering. "Looking at Jesus crucified," said one devout person, "makes the cross so lovable to me that I think I could never be happy without suffering; the love of Jesus Christ is all I need." Here is how Jesus advises everyone who would follow him: "Let them deny themselves and take up their cross daily" (Lk 9:23). But it must be taken up and carried, not by constraint or with repugnance, but with humility, patience, and love.

10 • Indeed, how much pleasure God has in those who humbly and patiently embrace the crosses that he sends them! Saint Ignatius of Loyola said, "There is no tree so apt to bring forth and maintain love for God as the tree of the holy cross,"[27] that is, to love him in the midst of sufferings. One day Saint Gertrude asked the Lord what was the most pleasing thing she could offer him; and he replied, "Daughter, you can do nothing more gratifying to me than to submit patiently to all the tribulations that come your way."[28] Thus the great servant of God, Sister Victoria Angelini, said that one day of crucifixion was worth a hundred years of all other spiritual exercises.[29] And the Venerable Father John of Ávila said, "One 'Blessed be God' in adversity is worth more than a thousand thanks in prosperity."[30] How sad it is, indeed, that so many people ignore the value of afflictions endured for God. Blessed Angela of Foligno used to say that if we knew what suffering for God really was, "it would become the target of robbery," meaning that everyone would try to rob others of the opportunity to suffer.[31] For this reason, Saint Mary Magdalen de Pazzi, knowing how precious suffering is, desired to have her life prolonged rather than to die and go to heaven, "because," said she, "in heaven one cannot suffer anymore."[32]

11 • A soul that loves God has no other goal but to be wholly united with him. But to reach this perfect union, let us listen to what Saint Catherine of Genoa said: "To achieve union with God, one must have adversities because God uses them to consume all our evil impulses within and without. And therefore insults, scorn, infirmities, abandonment by relatives and friends, confusions, temptations and other adversities are all supremely necessary, so that we can fight on, until, thanks to the victories, all our vile impulses will be extinguished within us so that we no longer feel them. And until all the adversities no longer seem bitter but sweet for God's sake, we shall never arrive at divine union."[33]

12 • Therefore a soul that desires to belong completely to God must be resolved, as Saint John of the Cross writes, not to seek out enjoyments in this life, but to suffer in all things,[34] eagerly embracing all voluntary mortifications, and with still more eagerness the involuntary ones, since those are more welcome to almighty God.

Solomon says, "One who is slow to anger is better than the mighty" (Prov 16:32). God is pleased by persons who practice mortification by fasting, hair shirts, and disciplines, because of the courage displayed in such mortifications; but he is much more pleased by those who have the courage to bear patiently and cheerfully the crosses that God sends them.

Saint Francis de Sales said, "The mortifications that come to us from God, or from fellow humans with God's permission, are always more precious than those born of our own will. It is a general rule that the less our own choice is involved, the more pleased God is, and the greater profit for ourselves."[35]

Saint Teresa of Ávila taught the same thing: "We gain more in one day from the afflictions visited on us by God or our neighbor than from ten years of self-inflicted suffering."[36] Saint Mary Magdalen de Pazzi generously declared that in the whole world there was no pain so bitter that she would not gladly bear it, thinking that it came from God. And, in fact, during the great trials that the saint suffered for five years, all it took to restore her peace of soul was to remind her that she was suffering because of the will of God.[37] In fact, to acquire this great treasure that is God, no price is too high! Father Ippolito Durazzo used to say, "However much God costs, the price is never too high."[38]

13 • Let us pray to God to make us worthy of his holy love; for if we were to love him perfectly, all the goods of this earth would seem to us smoke and dust, while pain and suffering would become our delight. Listen to what Saint John Chrysostom says about a soul wholly given to almighty God: "Those who have attained the perfect love of God seem to be alone on the earth. Such persons no longer care about either glory or shame. They scorn temptations and afflictions; they lose the taste and appetite for all things. And, not finding support or repose in anything, they continuously go about in search of their beloved without ever growing weary, so that when they work, when they eat, when they are awake or asleep, in every word and deed, all their thoughts and desires are to find their beloved; because in his heart is where treasure lies."[39]

In this chapter we have spoken about patience in general. In Chapter XIV we shall discuss particular situations where we especially have to exercise our patience.

Prayers of Love and Affection

Dearest and most beloved Jesus, my treasure, because of my offenses against you I do not deserve to be allowed to love you anymore. But thanks to your merits, I beg you, make me worthy of your pure love. I love you above all things; and I repent with my whole heart of having once despised you and driven you from my soul; but now I love you more than myself; I love you with all my heart, O infinite good! I repeat over and over again: I love you. I desire nothing more than to love you perfectly; nor do I fear anything except seeing myself deprived of your holy love.

My most loving Redeemer, make me know how great and good you are, and how great is the love you have borne me so as to make me love you.

My God, do not let me live any longer ungrateful to you for all your goodness! I have offended you enough, I do not ever want to leave you again; I wish to spend all the remaining years of my life loving you and pleasing you. My Jesus, my dearest love, help me; help a sinner who wishes to love you and to be all yours entirely.

O Mary, my hope, your son hears you; pray to him for me, and win for me the grace of loving him perfectly.

VI

"Love Is Kind": Those Who Love Jesus Christ Love Gentleness

1 • The spirit of gentleness is peculiar to God: "For the memory of me is sweeter than honey, and the possession of me sweeter than the honeycomb" (Sir 24:20). Hence souls that love God love all those who are loved by God, that is, our neighbors, so that they eagerly seek to help everyone, to console everyone, and, as far as they are able, to make everyone happy. Saint Francis de Sales, who was the master and model of holy gentleness, says, "Humble gentleness is the virtue of virtues that God has so much recommended to us; therefore we must practice it always and everywhere."[1] Thus the saint gives us this rule: "When you see that something can be done with love, do it; and when you see it cannot be done without quarreling, abandon it."[2] He means, of course, what can be left undone without offending God; because an offense against God must always be prevented, and as quickly as possible, by someone who is bound to prevent it.

2 • This gentleness should especially be practiced with the poor, who, by reason of their poverty, are generally given harsh treatment by others. It should likewise be particularly applied to the sick who are afflicted by disease, and who for the most part receive little assistance from the healthy. Gentleness is again especially called for in dealing with our enemies. "Do not be overcome by evil, but overcome evil with good" (Rom 12:21). Hatred must be overcome by love, and persecution by gentleness; that is what the saints did, and so they won over the affections of their most stubborn enemies.

3 • "There is nothing," says Saint Francis de Sales, "that so much edifies our neighbor as loving kindness."[3] Saints usually had smiles on their faces, radiating a kindliness that was expressed in their words and actions.[4] This led Saint Vincent de Paul to say of Francis de Sales that he had never known a kinder man. He said further that Monsignor de Sales seemed to him a vivid image of the kindliness of Jesus Christ.[5] Even when he had to refuse what he could not in conscience allow, he did so with such kindness that those he refused went away content and on good terms with him. He was gentle with everyone, with superiors, equals and inferiors, at home and outside[6]; unlike some people who, as the saint used to say, "seem angels outside the house, but demons at home."[7] In dealing with servants, he never complained of their failings; at most he would occasionally call their attention to it, but always with gentle words,[8] a very laudable thing and recommended to all superiors. Superiors should use every kindness toward their subordinates. When telling them what they have to do, they should request rather than command. Saint Vincent de Paul said, "There is no way for superiors to be better obeyed by their subordinates than through gentleness."[9] Similarly, Saint Jane Frances de Chantal said, "I have tried many methods of governing, but I have found none better than gentleness and tolerance."[10]

4 • Even when correcting faults, superiors should be kind. It is one thing to reprove forcefully, and another to rebuke harshly. Sometimes one must deliver a firm admonishment when the fault is serious, and especially if it be repeated after the subordinate's attention has been called to it. But let us always beware of harsh and angry rebukes; the person who chides with anger does more harm than good. This is that bitter zeal disapproved of by Saint James. Some people boast of keeping their family in line by the strict methods they use, claiming that this is how one must govern; but Saint James does not talk that way: "But if you have bitter envy and selfish ambition in your hearts, do not be boastful and false to the truth" (Jas 3:14). On some rare occasion it may be necessary to say a harsh word, to make the offender realize the gravity of the fault; still we should always leave the offender with a gentle expression and a few kind words. Wounds must be healed after the fashion of the Good Samaritan in the Gospel, with wine and oil: "Just as oil," said Saint Francis de Sales, "always swims on the surface of all other liquids, so must gentleness cover all our actions."[11] And if the person being corrected becomes disturbed, then the reproval must be put off till his anger subsides, or else we will only make things worse. The Canon Regular Saint John said: "When the house is on fire, one must not throw wood onto the flames."[12]

5 • "You know not of what spirit you are" (Lk 9:55; Vulgate). Such were the words of Jesus Christ to his disciples James and John when they called for fire from heaven to punish the Samaritans for expelling them from their village. Ah, the Lord said to them, what spirit is this? It is not my spirit, which is all gentle and kind, for "The Son of Man came not to destroy souls, but to save" (Lk 9:56; Vulgate). And would

you have me destroy them? Be quiet, and never ask me to do anything like that again, for this is not my spirit.

And, in fact, how gently Jesus Christ treated the woman taken in adultery! "Woman," he said, "where are they? Has no one condemned you?...Neither do I condemn you. Go your way, and from now on do not sin again" (Jn 8:10–11). He was content to warn her not to sin again, and sent her away in peace. Likewise, how gently he sought the conversion of the Samaritan woman, and so of course he did convert her. He first asked her to give him a drink; then he said to her: "If you knew...who it is that is saying to you, 'Give me a drink'" (Jn 4:10), and then he revealed to her that he was the longed-for Messiah. And, again, how gently did he try to convert the impious Judas, letting him eat from the same dish with him, washing his feet and admonishing him in the very act of his betrayal: "Judas, is it with a kiss that you are betraying the Son of Man?" (Lk 22:48). How, then, did he convert Peter after Peter denied him?

"The Lord turned and looked at Peter" (Lk 22:61). As he left the house of the high priest, without uttering a single reproach, he gave him a look of tenderness, and thus he converted him; and so effectively converted him that for as long as he lived Peter never ceased to lament the outrage he had done to his master.

6 • How much more is to be gained from gentleness than from bitterness! Saint Francis de Sales said there is nothing more bitter than the walnut, but when it is sugarcoated, it becomes sweet and agreeable: thus corrections, though in themselves displeasing, are made pleasant by love and gentleness, and so they prove more profitable.[13] Saint Vincent de Paul said of himself that in governing his congregation he had never corrected anyone harshly, except on three occasions, when he thought he had reason to do so; but he regretted it afterward, because those cases turned out badly, whereas he had always succeeded with gentleness.[14]

7 • Saint Francis de Sales got what he wanted from others with kindness; and in this way he managed to draw the most hardened sinners to God.[15] Saint Vincent de Paul took the same approach; he taught his disciples that, "Affability, love, and humility are wonderfully effective in winning the hearts of men, and in prevailing on them to embrace the things most repugnant to nature."[16] He once handed over a great sinner to the care of one of his Fathers, hoping to get him to repent, but, hard as he tried, the priest got nowhere and begged the saint to say a word to him. Saint Vincent accordingly spoke with him and converted him. The sinner later said that it was the peculiar gentleness and charity of Father Vincent that had won his heart. This was why the saint could not bear to have his missionaries treat sinners harshly: he told them that the devil exploits the strictness of some priests to work the greater ruin of souls.[17]

8 • Kindness should be practiced toward everyone, always and everywhere. Saint Bernard remarks that certain persons are gentle as long as things go their way; but no sooner do they meet with adversity or contradiction than they instantly flare up and began to smoke like Mount Vesuvius.[18] People like this might be compared to burning embers hidden beneath the ashes. Anyone who wishes to become a saint in this life must resemble the lily among thorns, which, however much it may be pricked by them, never ceases to be a lily; that is, it is always equally sweet and kind. Souls that love God

always maintain peace of heart; and they show this in their faces, always calm and steady regardless of what happens, in prosperity and adversity, as in the poem by Cardinal Pier Matteo Petrucci:[19]

> The soul sees how creatures change
> Their varied forms outside,
> But within, the deepest core
> Lives ever united and at one with God.

9 • Adversity shows what the spirit of a person is made of. Saint Francis de Sales dearly loved the Order of the Visitation, which had cost him so much labor to found. He often saw it in danger of going under because of the way it was persecuted; but the saint never lost his peace of mind. He would have been happy even were it to be destroyed, if God willed; and it was then that he said: "For some time now all the hostility and resistance that I have met with give me so sweet a peace that nothing can equal it, along with a foretaste of the anchoring of my soul in God, which is my only desire."[20]

10 • Whenever we have to reply to someone who is mistreating us, let us always take care to answer gently: "A soft answer turns away wrath" (Prov 15:1). A gentle reply is enough to quench every fire of anger. When we feel put out, it is better to keep silence, because then it seems right to say the first thing that comes to mind; but when our passion calms down, we see that what we said was wrong.

11 • And when it happens that we commit some fault, we must also be gentle with ourselves. Getting angry at ourselves after doing something wrong is not humility but a subtle form of pride, as if we were not the weak and wretched creatures that we are. Saint Teresa said: "The humility that unsettles comes not from God, but from the devil."[21] To be angry at ourselves after the commission of a fault is a greater fault than the one just committed, and it will lead to many others. It will make us abandon our devotions, prayers, and Communion; or if we do them, it will be done poorly. Saint Aloysius Gonzaga said that we cannot see in troubled waters, and that is where the devil goes fishing.[22]

When the soul is troubled, it loses sight of God and of what it has to do. So when we fall into any fault, we must turn to God with humility and confidence and, seeking his forgiveness, say to him, as Saint Catherine of Genoa used to say: "O Lord, these herbs come from my garden."[23] I love you with all my heart, and I repent of the displeasure I have given you. I don't want to do it again, give me your help.

Prayers of Love and Affection

Let us bless the chains that bind souls to God; let us pray that they grip us still more tightly that we can no longer loosen ourselves from the love of our God! My Jesus, I love you. I repeat, I love you, my treasure, my soul's very life; to you I cling, and I give myself completely to you. My beloved Lord, I never want to stop loving you again. You who paid for my sins by letting yourself be bound as a criminal, and thus bound to be led to death through the streets of Jerusalem—you who were willing to be nailed to the cross, and would not leave it until you had left your life there, oh, by the merit of all that pain, do not ever let be separated from you again!

Above every other evil, I regret that at one time I turned my back upon you; and with your grace I resolve to die rather than cause you any more displeasure, whether serious or slight.

My Jesus, I abandon myself to you. I love you with all my heart; I love you more than life itself. I have offended you in the past; but now I repent of it, and I would willingly die of grief. Draw me entirely to yourself.

I renounce all the consolations of the senses; I want you alone and nothing more. Make me love you, and then do with me what you will.

O Mary, my hope, bind me to Jesus; and make me always live bound to him and die bound to him, so as to come one day to the blessed kingdom, where I shall have no more fear of ever being torn from his holy love.

VII

"Love Is Not Jealous": The Soul That Loves Jesus Christ Does Not Envy the Great Ones of This World, but Only Those Who Are Greater Lovers of Jesus Christ

1 • Saint Gregory explains this next distinguishing mark of love when he says that love is not jealous, because it cannot find a reason to envy worldly people those kinds of earthly greatness that it despises rather than desires.[1] Hence we must distinguish between two kinds of emulation, one wicked and the other holy. The wicked kind envies, and is saddened by, the worldly goods that others possess on this earth. By contrast, holy emulation does not envy but rather pities the great ones of this world, who live amid honors and earthly pleasures. It seeks and desires nothing but God, and in this life it aims only to love him as much as possible; and therefore it has a holy envy of those who love him more than it does, for it would wish to surpass even the seraphim in loving him.

2 • This is the only goal of the saints on earth—a goal that so enamors and wounds the heart of God with love that it makes him say: "You have ravished my heart, my sister, my

bride, you have ravished my heart with one glance of your eyes" (Song 4:9). By "one glance" is meant the one purpose that souls wedded to the Lord have in all their exertions and thoughts, to please God. Worldly people in their actions look on things with many glances; that is, they have several disordered ends, such as to please others, to gain honor or riches and, if nothing else, to satisfy themselves. But the saints have a single glance, with which they look only to God's pleasure in all that they do. Along with David they say: "Whom have I in heaven but you? And there is nothing upon earth that I desire other than you....God is the strength of my heart and my portion for ever" (Ps 73:25–26). What else do I want, O my God, in this world or the next save you alone? You alone are my riches, you are the only Lord of my heart. "Let the rich," said Saint Paulinus, "enjoy their earthly treasures, let the kings enjoy their kingdoms. You, O Christ, are my treasure and my kingdom."[2]

3 • Hence we see that it is not enough to do good works, but we must do them well. For our works to be good and perfect, they must be done with the sole purpose of pleasing God. This was the worthy praise given to Jesus Christ: "He has done everything well" (Mk 7:37). Many actions would in themselves be praiseworthy, but because they are done with some other end in view than the glory of God, they are worth little or nothing to God. Saint Mary Magdalen de Pazzi said, "God rewards our actions according to the weight of their purity."[3] She meant that the Lord accepts and rewards our actions depending on how pure the intention is. But, dearest God, how hard it is to find an action done only for you! I remember a holy old religious, who had greatly toiled for God, and died with the reputation of a saint.[4] One day,

glancing back over his life, he was shaken by sadness and fear, and said, "O dear me! When I look at all the actions of my life, I cannot find one done entirely for God." How accursed is self-love, which costs all or the greater part of the fruit of our good actions! How many people even in the most sacred occupations—preachers, confessors, missionaries—labor and struggle, but gain little or nothing because they are not focused on God alone, but on worldly glory, or their own interests, or on the vanity of standing in the limelight, or simply on their own inclination!

4 • The Lord said: "Beware of practicing your piety before others in order to be seen by them; for then you have no reward from your Father in heaven" (Mt 6:1). "And whenever you pray, do not be like the hypocrites;...Truly, I tell you, they have received their reward" (Mt 6:5). But this reward comes down to a puff of smoke or a fleeting satisfaction that soon vanishes, leaving the soul empty-handed. The prophet Haggai says that whoever labors for any other reason except to please God is putting his reward in a bag full of holes, which, when he comes to open it, he will find empty: "You that earn wages earn wages to put them into a bag with holes" (Hag 1:6). That is why such people, if they fail to achieve the goal of their labors, are greatly disturbed. This is a sign that the glory of God had not been their sole object. Those who do something simply for the glory of God are not troubled at all by failure, because they have already achieved their purpose of pleasing God, by acting with a pure intention.

5 • Here are the signs that a person engaged in spiritual matters is working only for God: (1) if we are not bothered by the failure to reach our goals, because seeing that God does

not wish it, neither do we; (2) if we rejoice at the good done by others, as if we ourselves had done it; (3) if we do not desire one assignment more than another, but gladly accept whatever obedience to superiors entails; (4) if after our actions we seek neither thanks nor approval from others; and so, if others ever complain or disapprove, we will not be upset, but satisfied simply because we have pleased God. And if we should get some applause from the world, we do not get conceited, but meet the temptation to vanity as the Venerable John of Ávila did: "Go away; you have come too late. The work I did has already been given completely to God."[5]

6 • This is what is meant by entering into the joy of the Lord; that is, to enjoy God's own joy, as promised to his faithful servants: "Well done, good and trustworthy slave; you have been trustworthy in a few things, I will put you in charge of many things; enter into the joy of your master" (Mt 25:23). If we have the good fortune to do something that pleases God, what more, says Saint John Chrysostom, are we looking for? If you are found worthy to perform something that pleases God, what other compensation do you seek but this?[6] This is the greatest reward, the best piece of fortune that a creature can have: to give pleasure to its Creator.

7 • And that is what Jesus Christ expects from those that love him: "Set me," he says, "as a seal upon your heart; as a seal upon your arm" (Song 8:6). He wants them to place him as a seal on their hearts and on their arms: on the heart, so that whatever they plan on doing, they may intend solely for the love of God; on the arm, so that they may do whatever they do to please God, and that God may always be the only aim of all their thoughts and actions. Saint Teresa said that whoever wants to become a saint must live with no other desire than that of pleasing God.[7] And her eldest daughter, the Venerable Beatrice of the Incarnation, used to say, "There is no price high enough to pay for the slightest thing done for God."[8] And she was right, because all things done to please God are acts of love that unite us to God and win us eternal rewards.

8 • Purity of intention is known as the heavenly alchemy by which iron is turned into gold; that is, the most trivial actions, such as working, eating meals, recreating or resting, when done for God's sake, become the gold of holy love. That is why Saint Mary Magdalen de Pazzi took it for a certainty that those who do everything with a pure intention go straight to paradise, without passing through purgatory.[9] *The Spiritual Treasury* tells of a holy hermit who, before undertaking any action, used to pause for a moment and lift up his eyes to heaven. On being asked why he did so, he replied, "I am trying to make sure I hit the target."[10] He meant that, just as an archer, before shooting an arrow, takes aim at the target, so before doing anything he made God his aim, to be sure of pleasing him. We must do the same; and as we continue to carry out the work once begun, it is well for us from time to time to renew our intention of pleasing God.

9 • Those who have no other aim in their affairs but God's will enjoy the holy freedom of spirit proper to the children of God; and this lets them embrace everything that pleases Jesus Christ, however it may go against the grain of self-love or human respect. Love for Jesus Christ makes his lovers totally indifferent to what is sweet or bitter; they want nothing for their own pleasure, but everything for the pleasure

of God. They have the same peace of mind whether they are busied with great things or little things, with things pleasant or unpleasant: it is enough for them to please God.

10 • On the other hand, many people are willing to serve God, but it has to be in this or that assignment, in such and such a place, with certain companions and under certain circumstances, or else they will either quit the task or do it begrudgingly. Such persons have no freedom of spirit: they are slaves of self-love; and on that account profit little by what they do. They lead a restless life, because the yoke of Jesus Christ weighs heavily on them. The true lovers of Jesus Christ love to do with pure love only what pleases him and because it pleases him, when Jesus wills, where he wills, and as he wills, and whether he wishes them to occupy themselves in a life of worldly honor or in one of obscurity and neglect. What is important is loving him with a pure heart. This is the effort in which we must strive and toil, battling the appetites of self-love, which would like to see us busy in important posts that bring us honor and match our inclinations.

11 • We must also keep our distance from all activities, even spiritual ones, when the Lord wants us in other tasks more to his liking. One day, Father Álvarez, finding himself greatly overworked, wanted to hurry up and finish, so that he could go to pray, because he felt that during this time he wasn't with God. But then the Lord said to him: "Though I may not have you with me, I am making use of you—that should be enough."[11] This is a worthwhile lesson for persons who are sometimes upset when they are obliged, by obedience or the demands of charity, to leave their accustomed devotions. They should know that this sort of worry comes not from God, but either from the devil or from self-love. "Please God, and then go ahead and die"—that is the first maxim of the saints.

Prayers of Love and Affection

My eternal God, I offer you all my heart; but what sort of heart, O God, is it that I offer you? Though created to love you, it has many times rebelled against you. But look, my Jesus, if for a time my heart was rebellious, now it is deeply grieved and repentant for the displeasure it has given you. Yes, my dear Redeemer, I regret having valued you so little; and I am resolved to obey you, and to love you at all cost. I ask you to draw me wholly to your love, for the sake of the love that led you to die for me on the cross.

I love you, my Jesus; I love you with all my soul; I love you more than my very life. My only soul mate, none but you has sacrificed his life for love of me.

It makes me weep to think how ungrateful I have been to you. Pity me, I was already lost; but I hope that with your grace you have restored my life. And this shall be my life, to love you always, my sovereign good.

Make me love you, O source of infinite love, and I ask nothing more of you.

O Mary my mother, accept me as your servant, and win acceptance for me from Jesus your son.

VIII

"Love Does Not Deal Perversely": Those Who Love Jesus Christ Avoid Lukewarmness and Love Perfection, the Means to Which Are (1) Desire, (2) Resolution, (3) Meditation, (4) Communion, and (5) Prayer

1 • In explaining this phrase, "deals not perversely" (1 Cor 13:4; Vulgate), Saint Gregory says that love, as it devotes itself more and more exclusively to God, rejects whatever is not right and holy.[1] This is just what the apostle Paul wrote when he spoke about "love, which binds everything together in perfect harmony" (Col 3:14). And since love adores perfection, it naturally abhors the lukewarmness with which some persons serve God, thereby running a great risk of losing love, divine grace, their souls, and everything else.

2 • It must be noted that there are two kinds of lukewarmness: one kind is avoidable and the other not. Even the saints are subject to the latter sort, which comprises all the faults we commit without full consent, out of natural frailty. Such, for example, are distractions at prayer, inner disturbances, useless words, vain curiosity, the wish to show off, tastes in eating and drinking, the stirrings of concupiscence not instantly repressed, and so on. We ought to shun these faults as much as we can; but, owing to the weakness of our nature, which has been infected by sin, it is impossible to avoid them altogether. Still we ought to detest them once we have committed them, because they are displeasing to God; but, as we remarked in the previous chapter, we should beware of becoming upset by them. Saint Francis de Sales writes: "All thoughts that disturb us are not from God, who is the prince of peace; they always proceed from the devil, from self-love, or from the high estimation that we have of ourselves."[2]

3 • Such disturbing thoughts, therefore, must be immediately rejected and ignored. Saint Francis de Sales also said that indeliberate faults, which were committed involuntarily, are wiped out involuntarily.[3] An act of repentance, an act of love, is sufficient to cancel them. The Venerable Sister Maria Crocifissa, a Benedictine nun, saw once a globe of fire, on which a clump of straw was cast, immediately reducing it to ashes.[4] She was given to understand by this image that one fervent act of divine love destroys whatever defects we may have in our soul. The same effect is produced by holy Communion, as we are told by the Council of Trent, where the Eucharist is called "an antidote by which we are freed from daily faults."[5] Thus, such faults, though they are indeed faults, do not bar the way to perfection—that is, our making progress toward perfection; because in this life no one reaches perfection before getting to the kingdom of the blessed.

4 • Thus the tepidity that hinders perfection is avoidable when a person commits deliberate venial sins; because all these faults committed with open eyes can be effectively

avoided with the help of God's grace, even in this life. That is why Saint Teresa said: "May God deliver you from deliberate sin, however small it may be."[6] Such, for example, are willful lies, verbal attacks, cursing, bearing a grudge, mocking one's neighbor, cutting words, praising oneself, nursing rancor in one's heart, and inordinate attachments to persons of the opposite sex. "These are the sort of worms," Saint Teresa says, "which are not detected until they have gnawed their way into the virtues."[7] Hence, in another context, the saint observes: "The devil goes about using small things to make holes for great things to enter."[8]

5 • So we must fear such deliberate faults, since they lead God to withhold from us his brighter lights and stronger helps, and to deprive us of spiritual sweetness; and they make us perform all our spiritual exercises with great weariness and pain; and so, in course of time, we begin to abandon prayer, Communion, visits to the Blessed Sacrament, and novenas. In the end, we are likely to give up everything, as has often been the case with many unhappy souls.

6 • This is the meaning of the Lord's threat to the tepid: "You are neither cold nor hot. I wish that you were either cold or hot. So, because you are lukewarm...I am about to spit you out of my mouth" (Rev 3:15–16). Amazing! He says, "Would that you were cold"! How could that be? How could it be better to be cold, that is, deprived of grace, than to be lukewarm? Yes, in a certain sense it is better to be cold; because those persons who are cold may more readily change their lives, once they are stung by remorse. But those who are lukewarm get into the habit of drowsing away in their faults without repenting, or thinking of mending their ways, thus making their case

practically incurable. "Tepidity," writes Saint Gregory, "which has cooled down from fervor, is in desperate straits."[9] The Venerable Father L. da Ponte used to say that he had committed countless faults in his life, but that he had never made peace with them.[10] Some people sign a truce with their faults, and that brings about their ruin, especially when the fault is accompanied by some passion—self-esteem, the desire to show off, to accumulate money, resentment toward a neighbor, or inordinate affection for a person of the opposite sex. In such cases there is great danger, as Saint Francis of Assisi said, that bonds once as slight as hairs may turn into chains and drag the soul down to hell.[11] In all event, such souls will never become saints, and will forfeit the grand crowns that God was preparing for them, if they had been faithful to grace. No sooner does the bird feel released from the snare than it immediately flies away: as soon as it is freed from earthly attachments, the soul immediately flies off to God. But if it is bound, a single thread will be enough to prevent it from making its way to God. How many spiritual persons fail to become saints, because they will not force themselves to break away from certain little attachments!

7 • All the harm arises from the lack of love they have for Jesus Christ. Those who are puffed up with self-esteem, those who are often heartbroken by events that go against the grain of their desires, who coddle themselves because of their health, whose hearts are wide open to external objects, and whose minds are always distracted, keen to hear and to know so many things that have nothing to do with the service of God, but only with their personal satisfaction, who resent every little imaginary slight from others, which often leads them to grow troubled and remiss in prayer and recollection. One

moment they are all devout and jubilant, the next all impatient and sad, depending on whether things are going their way or not. They do not love Jesus Christ or love him very little, and give true devotion a bad name.

8 • But if one were to fall into this wretched state of tepidity, what is to be done about it? Certainly it is a hard thing for a soul grown lukewarm to recover its old fervor; but our Lord has said, "What is impossible for mortals is possible for God" (Lk 18:7). Those who pray and take the necessary means will achieve everything they desire.

There are five means for escaping tepidity and setting out on the path of perfection:

1. The desire of perfection
2. The resolution to attain it
3. Meditation
4. Frequent holy Communion
5. Prayer

9 • The first means is the desire of perfection. Holy desires are the wings that lift us up from the earth; for, as Saint Laurence Giustiniani says, desire "supplies strength and makes pain easier to bear."[12] On the one hand, it gives us the energy to take the path to perfection; and on the other hand it lightens the fatigue of the journey. Those who really desire perfection never stop advancing toward it; and if they don't give up, they finally get there. On the contrary, those who don't desire it will always go backward and always find themselves more imperfect than before. Saint Augustine says, "On the road to God not to go forward is to go backward."[13] Those who make no effort to advance will always find themselves behind, swept away by the current of our corrupt nature.

10 • So it is a great mistake to say, "God doesn't want everyone to be a saint." On the contrary, Saint Paul says, "For this is the will of God, your sanctification" (1 Thes 4:3). God wants all of us to be saints, and each one according to his or her state of life: the religious as a religious, laypeople as laypeople, the priest as a priest, the married person as married, the merchant as merchant, the soldier as a soldier, and so on, in every other state of life.

I have some beautiful material on this subject from my great patroness, Saint Teresa. She says, in one place, "Our thoughts should be grand; that way lies our good."[14] Elsewhere she says: "We must not lower our expectations, but trust in God, so that by pressing ourselves we may gradually get to the point where, by God's grace, so many saints have gotten."[15] And in confirmation of this she cites her own experience that courageous souls make great progress in a short period of time.[16] This, she says, is because "the Lord takes as much delight in our desires as if they were already carried out." In another context she says: "God does not confer extraordinary favors except to those who have greatly desired his love." Again, in another passage, she remarks: "God never fails to repay every good desire in this life; for he is the friend of generous souls, provided that they have a healthy distrust of themselves." The saint herself was endowed with just this sort of generous spirit, which once led her to tell the Lord that were she to see others in paradise enjoying him more than herself, she wouldn't mind; but were she to see anyone loving him more, she didn't know how she could endure it.[17]

11 • So we must be greatly encouraged: "The Lord is good to those who wait for him, to the soul that seeks him" (Lam

3:25). God is surpassingly good and generous to souls that seek him with all their hearts. Nor, if we really desire to become saints, can our past sins prevent us. Saint Teresa remarks: "The devil strives to make it look like pride when we have great desires and wish to imitate the saints; but it is very useful to build up our courage to do great things; because, although the soul may not immediately have the strength, it still launches out on a bold fight and makes rapid advances."[18]

The apostle Paul writes: "We know that all things work together for good for those who love God" (Rom 8:28). And to "everything" an ancient commentary adds "even sins." Even the sins we have committed can play a part in our sanctification, insofar as the memory of them makes us humbler and more grateful, when we see the favors that God lavishes on us after we have so greatly offended him. I can do nothing, the sinner should say, and I deserve anything; I deserve nothing but hell. But I am dealing with a God of infinite goodness, who has promised to listen to all who pray to him. Now that he has rescued me from the state of damnation and wishes me to become a saint, and now that he is offering me his help, I certainly can become a saint, not by my own powers, but by the grace of my God, who strengthens me: "I can do all things through him who strengthens me" (Phil 4:13). Thus, since we do have good desires, we must take courage and, trusting in God, endeavor to carry them out. But if afterward we encounter an obstacle in any spiritual enterprise, let us find calm in God's will. Whatever God wants must be preferred to every good desire we may have. Saint Mary Magdalen de Pazzi said she preferred to lack any perfection than to have it without the will of God.[19]

12 • The second means of perfection is the resolution to give oneself completely to God.

Many are called to perfection; they are urged on to it by grace, they conceive a desire for it. But then because they never really resolve to seek it, they live and die in the stench of their tepid and imperfect lives. The desire for perfection is not enough, there must be a firm resolution to attain it. Many souls feel desires, but never take a step on the path to God. These are the desires that the wise person speaks of when saying: "The craving of the lazy person is fatal, for lazy hands refuse to labor" (Prov 21:25). Lazy people are forever desiring, but they never resolve to take the measures needed, given their way of life, to become a saint. They say: "Oh, if only I could live in another monastery, I would give myself entirely to God!" And meanwhile they can't endure this or that companion; they can't put up with a word of contradiction; they are distracted by many useless cares; they commit a thousand faults of gluttony, curiosity, and pride; and yet they sigh to the wind: "Oh, if only I had..." or "Oh, if only I could...," and so on. Such desires do more harm than good; because some people regale themselves with them, and in the meantime go on living a life of imperfection. Saint Francis de Sales used to say: "I don't approve of people who, once they are committed to some duty or vocation, stop to long for another kind of life, unsuited to their position, or for other exercises incompatible with their present state. This distracts their heart, and makes them mope about in their necessary duties."[20]

13 • We must, therefore, desire perfection and resolutely take the means to achieve it. Saint Teresa says: "God asks for no more from us than a single resolution, afterwards he will do the rest himself. The devil has no fear of irresolute souls."[21]

That is the purpose of meditation, to lay hold of the means that lead to perfection. Some people pray a great deal, but never come to any sort of conclusion." The same saint said: "I would prefer a short prayer that has great results to a prayer lasting many years, in which a soul never manages to resolve to do something worthy for God."[22] And elsewhere she says: "I have learned by experience that if one helps oneself from the outset by resolving to do something, however difficult, if it be done to please God, then there is nothing to fear."[23]

14 • The first resolution must be to make every effort and to die rather than commit any deliberate sin, however small. It is true that without God's help all our efforts are not enough to overcome temptations. But God often wants us to use force on ourselves, because then he will make up for our weakness with his grace and enable us to win the victory. This resolution frees us from every obstacle to moving ahead; and, at the same time, gives us great courage, because it assures us that we are in God's grace. Saint Francis de Sales writes: "The best guarantee we can have in this world of being in the grace of God is not the feelings that we have of his love, but the pure and irrevocable abandonment of our whole being into his hands and in the firm resolve never to consent to any sin, either great or small."[24]

This means having a delicate conscience. It should be noted that it is one thing to have a delicate conscience and quite another to be scrupulous. Delicacy of conscience is needed to become a saint; but scrupulousness is a fault and does harm. That is why we must obey our spiritual director and conquer scruples, which are nothing but vain and senseless apprehensions.

15 • Hence one must resolve to choose the best, not only what is pleasing to God, but what is most pleasing to him, without reserve. Saint Francis de Sales says: "We must start with a strong and steady resolution to give ourselves wholly to God, and proclaim to him that in the future we want to be his without reservation; and then we must often renew this same resolution."[25] Saint Andrew Avellino took a vow to make progress toward perfection every day.[26] Those who wish to become a saint need not take a vow; but every day they must try to make some progress toward perfection. Saint Laurence Giustiniani has written: "When a person is really making headway, there is felt a continual longing to advance; and the more perfection grows, the more this longing for advancement grows; because as the interior light grows brighter each day, it always seems to the person wishing to progress that he or she is lacking in every virtue and that no good is being done at all. And if one is aware of doing some good, it always seems highly imperfect to that person, and little is made of the effort. The upshot is that this person is continually working to acquire perfection without ever feeling tired."[27]

16 • We must begin promptly and not wait till tomorrow. Who knows whether or not we will have the time. Ecclesiastes observes: "Whatever your hand finds to do, do with your might" (Eccl 9:10). Whatever you can do, do it quickly, and do not put it off. And he gives the reason why: "For there is no work or thought or knowledge or wisdom in Sheol, to which you are going" (Ibid.). In the next life there will be no more time to work, nor grounds for merit, nor wisdom to do well, nor knowledge or experience to think things over carefully, because after death what is done is done.

A nun named Sister Bonaventura, from the convent of

Torre de' Specchi in Rome, had been leading a very lukewarm sort of life. Then a religious, Father Lancisio, came to give the Spiritual Exercises to the nuns; and Sister Bonaventura, who felt no inclination to shake off her tepidity, began to listen to the exercises against her will. But at the very first sermon she was won over by divine grace, so that she immediately went to Father Lancisio and said to him, with real determination, "Father, I wish to become a saint—quickly." And, with God's help, she did so; for she lived only eight months afterward, and in that brief time she lived and died a saint.[28]

17 • David says: "And I said, now have I begun" (Ps 76:11; Vulgate). In the same vein Saint Charles Borromeo declared: "Today I begin to serve God."[29] And that is how we should act, as if in the past we had done no good whatever. For, indeed, all that we do for God *is* nothing, since we are bound to do it. Let us therefore resolve each day that we will begin to belong wholly to God. But let us pay no attention to what others do or how they do it. Those who truly become saints are few in number. Saint Bernard says: "One cannot be perfect without being different."[30] If we wish to imitate the common run of humankind, we shall always remain imperfect, as they generally are. We must overcome everything and renounce everything, in order to gain everything. Saint Teresa said: "Ultimately we don't give all our love to God, and so he doesn't give us all his either."[31]

Let us remember how little is done for Jesus Christ, who has given his blood and his life for us. "Whatever we can do," says the same saint, "is foulness in comparison with one single drop of blood shed for us by the Lord."[32] The saints never spare themselves when it is a question of pleasing the God who gave himself completely and unreservedly to us, just to oblige us to deny him nothing. Saint John Chrysostom writes: "He gave everything to you, and kept nothing for himself."[33] God has given his whole self to you; there is no excuse for you to hold back anything from God. As the apostle Paul says, "And he died for all, so that those who live might live no longer for themselves, but for him who died and was raised for them" (2 Cor 5:15).

18 • The third means of becoming a saint is *meditation.* Jean de Gerson writes that those who do not meditate on the eternal truths cannot, without a miracle, live as Christians.[34] This is because without mental prayer, light is missing, and we walk in darkness. The truths of faith are not seen by the eyes of the body, but by the eyes of the soul when we meditate. Those who do not meditate on them, fail to see them, and therefore walk in the dark. Hence they easily become attached to sensible objects, for the sake of which they despise what is eternal. Saint Teresa writes (Letter 8) to the bishop of Osma: "Although it seems to us that we have no imperfections, yet when God opens the eyes of the soul, as he is wont to do in prayer, then they appear plainly enough."[35] And Saint Bernard earlier said that he who does not meditate "does not abhor himself, simply because he does not know himself."[36] "Prayer," says the saint, "rules our emotions and directs our acts (toward God),"[37] but without prayer our affections become attached to the earth, our actions are shaped by our affections, and everything turns chaotic.

19 • We read of a dreadful instance of this in the life of the Venerable Sister Maria Crocifissa of Sicily. Once while the servant of God was praying, she heard a devil boasting that he had succeeded in making a nun give up community prayer. She saw in spirit that after tripping her up in this way, the devil was tempting her to consent to a grievous sin; and she was on the point of yielding. Sister Maria immediately rushed to her side, admonished her, and prevented her from falling.[38] Saint Teresa says that anyone who quits praying "soon becomes either a beast or a devil."[39]

20 • Therefore those who give up prayer will give up loving Jesus Christ. Prayer is the blessed furnace in which the fire of holy love is kindled and kept alive. Saint Catherine of Bologna said: "Anyone who stops praying cuts the string binding the soul to God. Then the devil, finding the soul cold in divine love, will induce it to taste of some poisoned apple."[40] On the other hand, as Saint Teresa said, "I am sure than anyone who perseveres in prayer, no matter how many sins the devil may charge that person with, will eventually see the Lord bring him into the haven of salvation."[41] In another place she says: "Those who do not halt on the way of prayer will get there sooner or later."[42] And elsewhere she writes that the devil works so hard to deter souls from prayer, because, "He knows that the soul that perseveres in prayer is lost to him."[43]

How many good things come to us through prayer! In prayer we conceive holy thoughts, we feel devout affections, we are stirred to great desires, and make firm resolutions to give ourselves wholly to God; thus, for his sake, the soul sacrifices earthly pleasures and all disorderly appetites. Saint Aloysius Gonzaga said, "There will never be much perfection without much prayer."[44] Those who long for perfection should mark this saying.

21 • We should not pray to taste the sweet joys of divine love; those who pray from such a motive will waste their time or profit little from it. People should betake themselves to prayer only to please God, that is, only to learn what God wants from them and to beg his help to put it into practice. The Venerable Father Antonio Torres said: "Carrying the cross without consolation makes souls fly to perfection."[45] Prayer without sensible consolations proves to be most fruitful for the soul. But how poor the soul who gives up prayer, because it finds no pleasure in its practice. Saint Teresa said: "When souls give up prayer, it is as if they were flinging themselves into hell without any need of devils."[46]

22 • The practice of prayer, then, leads a person to think constantly of God. "The true lover," says Saint Teresa, "is always mindful of the beloved."[47] That is why persons who pray are always talking about God, because they know how pleased God is when his lovers take delight in speaking of him and in the love he bears them, and when they try to spread its flame to others. The same saint writes: "Jesus Christ is always present in the conversations of the servants of God, and he is much pleased that they delight in him."[48]

23 • Prayer is also the source of the desire to withdraw into solitary places and converse by oneself with God, and to maintain a state of inner recollection while handling necessary external duties. By "necessary" I mean such things as the management of one's family or the performance of duties required of us by obedience, because a person of prayer must love solitude, and not become lost in willful and useless affairs. Otherwise he or she will lose the spirit of recollection, which is a crucial means of preserving union with God: "A garden locked is my sister, my bride" (Song 4:12). The soul wedded to Jesus Christ must be a garden closed off to all creatures, and must not ad-

mit into its heart other thoughts or other affairs than those of or for God. Hearts left open do not become holy. The saints, who are workers, winning souls for God, stay recollected amid their labors, whether preaching, hearing confessions, making peace, or helping the sick. The same is true for those who have to apply themselves to study. How many people, for all their efforts to study hard and acquire learning, become neither holy nor learned, because true learning is the knowledge of the saints, that is, learning how to love Jesus Christ; whereas, on the contrary, divine love brings with it both knowledge and every good: "All good things came to me along with her" (Wis 7:11), that is, with holy love.

Saint John Berchmans had an extraordinary love of study, but he never let his studies get in the way of his spiritual interests.[49] The apostle Paul writes: "I say to everyone among you not to think of yourself more highly than you ought to think, but to think with sober judgment" (Rom 12:3). This is true of everyone, but especially of priests, because they have to instruct others in God's law: "For the lips of a priest should guard knowledge, and people should seek instruction from his mouth" (Mal 2:7). Priests must have knowledge, but "with sober judgment." Those who abandon prayer for study show that they are not seeking God in their study but themselves. Those who seek God leave off their studies, unless they are necessary just then, so as not to leave off prayer.

24 • The worst of it is that without mental prayer, we do not pray at all. In many passages of my spiritual works, I have spoken about the necessity of prayer, and more especially in a little volume entitled *On the Grand Means of Prayer*; and in the present chapter I shall also briefly discuss a few more aspects of it. Here let me just quote the opinion of the Venerable Monsignor Giovanni de Palafox, bishop of Osma, in his remarks on the letters of Saint Teresa: "How can charity last, unless God gives us perseverance? How will the Lord give us perseverance unless we ask him for it? And how shall we ask him for it except through prayer? Without prayer there is no communication with God to preserve our virtues."[50] And this is true, because those who do not meditate have little insight into the needs of their soul; they have little awareness of the dangers to their salvation or of the means to be used for overcoming temptations; and so, barely realizing the necessity of prayer, they abandon it and will surely be lost.

25 • As regards subjects for meditation, nothing is more useful than to reflect on the four Last Things—death, judgment, hell, and heaven. But it is especially worthwhile to meditate on death, and to imagine ourselves on our deathbed holding a crucifix and on the point of entering into eternity. But above all, for those who love Jesus Christ and desire to keep growing in his love, no thought is more powerful than that of the Passion of the Redeemer. Saint Francis de Sales said, "Mount Calvary is the mountain of lovers."[51] All the lovers of Jesus Christ wish to dwell on this mountain, where the only air they breathe is the air of divine love. When we see a God who dies for our love ("Christ loved us and gave himself up for us" [Eph 5:2]), it is impossible not to love him ardently. From the wounds of Christ crucified, arrows of love continually shoot forth to pierce even hearts of stone. Happy are those who in this life are continually climbing up Calvary! Let us bless this mountain, this lovely and beloved mountain! Who would ever leave you, O mountain that sends forth fire and inflames the souls that persevere and abide on you!

26 • The fourth means of perfection and of perseverance in the grace of God is frequent Communion, of which we have already spoken in Chapter II, where we said that a soul can do nothing more pleasing to Jesus Christ than to receive him often in the sacrament of the altar.

Saint Teresa says, "There is no better help to perfection than frequent Communion: oh, how admirably does the Lord use it to bring souls to perfection!" And she adds that, ordinarily speaking, those who receive Communion most often are more advanced toward perfection, and that the spirit reigns more in monasteries where frequent Communion is the custom.[52] This is why, as we read in a decree of Innocent XII from the year 1679, the holy Fathers so extolled and promoted the practice of frequent and even of daily Communion.[53] Holy Communion, as the Council of Trent tells us, delivers us from everyday faults and preserves us from mortal ones.[54] Saint Bernard says that Communion represses the stirrings of anger and lust, which are the two passions that most frequently and most violently assault us.[55] Saint Thomas says that Communion defeats the suggestions of the devil.[56] And finally, Saint John Chrysostom writes that Communion instills in us a strong inclination to virtue and a readiness to practice it, and at the same time bestows on us a great peace, which makes the path of perfection sweet and easy to us.[57] Above all, no other sacrament so inflames souls with divine love as the sacrament of the Eucharist, in which Jesus Christ gives us his whole self, so to unite us all to him through holy love. Thus the Venerable Father John of Ávila said: "Whoever deters souls from frequent Communion is doing the work of the devil."[58] Indeed, for the devil has a great horror of this sacrament, from which souls derive great strength to advance in divine love.

27 • To receive Communion well one must make a suitable preparation. The first, or remote, preparation is (1) to abstain from all deliberate faults, that is, from sinning with open eyes; (2) the practice of frequent mental prayer; and (3) the mortification of the senses and of the passions.

In his *Introduction to the Devout Life* Saint Francis de Sales teaches that "whoever has overcome most of his evil inclinations and has reached a notable level of perfection can receive Communion every day."[59] Saint Thomas Aquinas says that anyone may take daily Communion, if he or she has learned that communicating increases the fervor of holy love."[60] That is why Innocent XII, in the decree just mentioned, says that the greater or lesser frequency of Communion should be determined by the confessor, to the extent that he sees the souls under his direction profiting from it.

The proximate preparation for Communion is made on the same morning on which one receives the sacrament, and it requires at least half an hour of mental prayer.

28 • In addition, in order to reap a rich harvest from Communion we must make a long thanksgiving. Father John of Ávila writes that the time after Communion is "a time to gain treasures of graces."[61] Saint Mary Magdalen de Pazzi used to say that no time is better suited to inflame us with divine love than the time after Communion.[62] And Saint Teresa says: "After Communion let us not waste so good an opportunity to do business with God. As a rule, His Divine Majesty does not pay badly for his lodging, if he gets a good reception."[63]

29 • There are certain fainthearted souls, who, on being urged to communicate more frequently, reply: "But I'm not worthy." Do you not know that the longer you go without taking Communion, the more you render yourself unworthy of it? Without Communion, you will have less strength, and you will commit more sins. Come now, obey your director and follow his guidance. Venial sins are no obstacle to Communion when they are not fully voluntary. Besides, among your faults, the greatest is this: not doing what your spiritual father tells you to do.

30 • "But in the past I led a bad life." To which I reply, "Don't you know that the sickest person has most need of the doctor and of medicine." Jesus in the Blessed Sacrament is both our doctor and our medicine. Saint Ambrose said: "I, who am always sinning, must always have my medicine."[64] You may say: "But my confessor doesn't tell me to receive Communion more often." If he doesn't, ask his permission. If he refuses, obey, but in the meantime make the request. "But it looks like pride." It would be pride, if you wished to take Communion contrary to his opinion, but not when you humbly ask it of him. This heavenly bread requires hunger. Jesus loves to be desired, says a devout author: "He thirsts to be thirsted for."[65] And then the thought, "Today I have communicated, and tomorrow I have to communicate," alerts the soul to avoid all faults and to do the will of God. "But I have no fervor." If you mean sensible fervor, that is not necessary, nor does God always grant it even to his beloved souls. The only fervor you need is the will to belong completely to God and to advance in his divine love. Jean de Gerson says that those who abstain from Communion because they don't feel the devotion they would like to feel act like people who stay away from the fire because they don't feel warm.[66]

31 • My God, many souls stop asking for holy Communion, as not to commit themselves to living in a more recollected state and at a greater distance from worldly things. And this is the real reason why they don't want to receive Communion more often. They realize that frequent Communion doesn't go together with the wish to show off, with vanity in dressing, with attachment to gluttony, comforts, and amusing conversations: they know that it calls for more prayer, more inner and outer mortifications, more seclusion. And that is why they are ashamed to approach the altar more often. There is no doubt it is well for such souls to abstain from frequent Communion, since they find themselves in such a wretched state of tepidity and indifference. But that state is one that sooner or later those called to a more perfect life must get out of, unless they wish to endanger their eternal salvation.

32 • Again it helps a great deal, if one wants to keep the soul fervent, to make frequent spiritual Communion. The custom is highly praised by the Council of Trent, which exhorts all the faithful to practice it.[67] Spiritual Communion, as Saint Thomas says, consists in a burning desire to receive Jesus Christ in the sacrament[68]; and therefore the saints wished to make it several times a day. One prays more or less as follows: "My Jesus, I believe that you are really present in the Most Holy Sacrament. I love you, and I desire you; come into my soul. I embrace you; and I beg you, never let me be separated from you again." Or, more briefly: "My Jesus, come to me; I desire you; I embrace you; let us remain forever united." This spiritual Communion may be practiced several times a day: when we say our prayers, when we make a visit to the Blessed Sacrament, and especially at the moment of the priest's Communion when we attend Mass. The Dominican nun, Blessed Agatha of the

Cross, said: "If my confessor had not taught me this method of communicating spiritually several times a day, I don't know how I would have survived."[69]

33 • The fifth and most necessary means for the spiritual life and for obtaining the love of Jesus Christ is *prayer.*

In the first place, I say that by this means God shows us the great love he bears us. What greater proof of affection can a person give to a friend than to say to him, "My friend, ask me to give you anything you want, and you will get it"? Now that is precisely what the Lord tells us: "Ask, and it will be given you; search, and you will find" (Lk 11:9). Hence prayer is said to be all-powerful with God to obtain every blessing: "Prayer, though it is only one thing, can accomplish all things," as Theodoretus says.[70] Those who pray obtain from God whatever they want. The words of David are beautiful: "Blessed be God, because he has not rejected my prayer, or removed his steadfast love from me" (Ps 66:20). Commenting on this passage, Saint Augustine says, "As long as you see that you are not failing in prayer, rest assured that God's mercy will not fail you either."[71] And Saint John Chrysostom adds: "We always get an answer, even while we are still praying."[72] When we pray to God, even before we finish, he grants us the grace we seek. Thus if we are poor, we have only ourselves to blame, because we want to be poor, and so we don't deserve pity. What sympathy can there be for a beggar who has a very rich master, and one eager to supply him with everything if he will only ask for it, but who nevertheless chooses to continue in his poverty rather than ask for what he needs? Look, says the apostle Paul, our God is ready to enrich all who call upon him: "The same Lord is Lord of all and is generous to all who call on him" (Rom 10:12).

34 • Humble prayer, then, obtains everything from God; but we must realize at the same time that, useful as it is, it is also indispensable for our salvation. We absolutely require God's help to overcome temptations. And sometimes, in the face of more violent assaults, the sufficient grace that God gives everyone would be enough for us to resist them; but on account of our inclination to evil, it is not, and we need a special grace. Those who pray receive it; but those who don't pray, don't receive it, and are lost. And speaking in particular about the grace of final perseverance, of dying in the grace of God, which is the grace absolutely necessary for our salvation, and without which we should be lost forever, Saint Augustine says that God bestows this grace only on those who pray for it.[73] And that is the reason why so few are saved, because so few bother to beg God for the grace of perseverance.

35 • To sum up, the holy Fathers say that prayer is necessary for us, not merely as a precept (the Fathers of the Church say that those who let a month go by without commending their eternal salvation to God are not exempt from mortal sin) but also as a means, that is to say, whoever does not pray cannot possibly be saved. And the reason for this, in short, is that we cannot obtain salvation without the help of God's grace, and God gives such grace only to those who pray. And because temptations and the dangers of falling into disgrace with God continuously beset us, our prayers must be continuous too. Hence Saint Thomas writes that continuous prayer is necessary for salvation.[74] Jesus Christ said it first: "And Jesus told them a parable about their need to pray always and not to lose heart" (Lk 18:1). Hence the apostle Paul says: "Pray without ceasing" (1 Thes 5:17). No sooner do we stop making our case with God than the devil conquers us. And though, as the Council of Trent teaches, we can never deserve the grace of perseverance,[75] nevertheless Saint Augustine says that "in a certain sense it can be merited by prayer."[76] The Lord wants to dispense his grace to us, but he wants to be asked. Indeed, as Saint Gregory says, he wants to be importuned and, in a manner, constrained by our prayers.[77] Saint Mary Magdalen de Pazzi said, "When we ask grace of God, he not only hears us, but in a certain sense he graciously thanks us."[78] Since God is infinite goodness who wishes to pour himself out upon others, he has, as it were, an infinite longing to distribute his gifts to us. But he wants to be asked: so when he sees himself entreated by a soul, he gets so much pleasure that in a manner of speaking he thanks the soul for it.

36 • Thus, if we wish to remain in God's grace till death, we must play the part of beggars and keep our mouths open to pray for God's help, always repeating, "My Jesus, mercy; do not let me be separated from you. O Lord, come to my aid. My God, help me!" This was the unceasing prayer of the ancient Fathers of the desert: "Be pleased, O God, to deliver me. O Lord, make haste to help me!" (Ps 70:1). Lord, help me, and help me quickly, for if you delay with your assistance, I shall fall and perish. We must do this above all in time of temptation; otherwise we shall be lost.

37 • And let us have great faith in prayer. God has promised to hear those who pray: "Ask, and you will receive" (Jn 16:24). How can we doubt, says Saint Augustine, since God has bound himself by express promise and cannot fail to grant us the favors we ask of him?[79] In commending ourselves to God, we must have the sure confidence that God hears us, and then we shall obtain whatever we want. Here is what Jesus Christ says: "Whatever you ask for in prayer, believe that you have received it, and it will be yours" (Mk 11:24).

38 • "But," someone may say, "I am a sinner, and I do not deserve to be heard." Jesus Christ says: "For everyone who asks receives" (Lk 11:10). That means all of us, the sinners as well as the just. Saint Thomas teaches us that the power of prayer to obtain graces does not depend on our merits, but on the mercy of God, who has promised to hear everyone who prays to him.[80] And our Savior, to free us from all fear when we pray, told us: "Very truly, I tell you, if you ask anything of the Father in my name, he will give it to you" (Jn 16:23). It is as if he were saying: Sinners, you have no merits of your own to obtain grace. So when you would obtain grace, ask it of my Father in my name, that is, through my merits and through my love; and then ask for as much as you want, and it will be granted to you. But mark well the phrase, "in my name," which means (as Saint Thomas explains) "in the name of the Savior" or, in other words, that the grace we ask for must relate to our eternal salvation.[81] The Lord's promise has nothing to do with temporal favors: when they are good for our eternal welfare, he grants them; when they are not, he denies them. So we should always ask for temporal favors on condition that they benefit our soul. But when what we want are spiritual graces, no conditions are required. We should simply say with confidence, and a sure confidence: "Eternal Father, in the name of Jesus Christ deliver me from this temptation, give me holy perseverance, give me your love, give me paradise." This is the sort of grace we can ask of Jesus Christ in his own name, that is, through his merits, since here his promise applies: "If in my name you ask me for anything, I will do it" (Jn 14:14). And when we pray to God, let us also remember to commend ourselves to Mary, the dispenser of graces. Saint Bernard says that it is almighty God who gives the grace, but he distributes it through the hands of Mary: "Let us seek grace, and let us seek it through Mary; because what she seeks she finds, and she cannot be refused."[82] If Mary prays for us, we are safe; for all Mary's prayers are heard, they are never turned down.

Prayers of Love and Affection

Jesus, my love, I am determined to love you as much as I can, and I want to become a saint. I want to become a saint to give you pleasure and to love you greatly in this life and the next. I can do nothing by myself, but you can do all things; and I know that you want me to become a saint. I can already see that because of your grace my soul sighs only for you and seeks no one but you. I no longer wish to live for myself; you desire me to be wholly yours, and I desire to be wholly yours. Come and join me to yourself, and yourself to me. You are infinite goodness; you are the one who has loved me so much. You are, therefore, most loving and most lovable. How, then, can I love anything but you? I prefer your love to everything in this world. You are the only object, the only goal of all my affections. I abandon everything, so as to be wholly absorbed in loving you, my Creator, my Redeemer, my consolation, my love, my everything.

I will not despair of becoming a saint because of the offenses of my past life. I know, my Jesus, that you died to pardon those who truly repent. I love you now with my whole heart, with my whole soul; I love you more than myself, and I regret, more than any other evil, having despised you, my sovereign good.

Now I am no longer my own, I am yours, God of my heart, dispose of me as you wish. In order to please you, I accept all the tribulations you wish to send me: sickness, sorrow, distress, ignominy, poverty, persecution, desolation. I accept it all to please you, just as I accept the death you have prepared for me, with all the anguish and trials that may accompany it. Just grant me the grace to love you greatly. Lend me your help; give me the strength, with my love, to compensate in what is left of my life for all the bitterness that I caused you before, the only love of my soul.

O Queen of Heaven, O Mother of God, O great advocate of sinners, I put my trust in you.

IX

"Love Is Not Boastful": Those Who Love Jesus Christ Are Not Vain About Their Own Worth, but Humble Themselves, and Are Glad to Be Humbled by Others

1 • The proud person is like a balloon filled with air, which seems great to itself, but whose whole greatness, in reality, comes down to a little wind, which, as soon as the balloon is opened, is quickly dissipated. Those who love God are humble and are not puffed up by seeing any worth in themselves, because they know that whatever they have is a gift of God, and that of themselves they have only nothingness and sin. Thus the knowledge of the divine favors bestowed on them humbles them all the more, seeing how unworthy they are and yet so favored by God.

2 • In speaking of the special favors she received from God, Saint Teresa says, "God treats me as if I were a house that is about to tumble down: he props me up."[1] When souls receive a loving visit from God, and feel an unusual warmth of divine love, accompanied with tears or great tenderness of heart, let them beware of supposing that the Lord is favoring them in reward for some good deed. Instead they should humble themselves all the more and think that God cherishes them in order that they may not forsake him. Otherwise, were they to flatter themselves because of such favors, imagining themselves more privileged because they were on better terms with God than others, such a fault would make God deprive them of his favors. The two things most necessary to hold a house together are the foundation and the roof. The foundation in us must be humility, in acknowledging that we are good for nothing and capable of nothing; and the roof is God's help, in which alone we ought to put our trust.

3 • Whenever we see ourselves more favored by God, we must humble ourselves that much more. When Saint Teresa received some special grace, she strove to keep before her eyes all the faults she had ever committed; and thus the Lord bound her more closely to himself.[2] The more souls confess themselves undeserving of any favors, the more God enriches them with his grace. Thaïs, who was first a sinner and then a saint, humbled herself so profoundly before God that she thought herself unworthy even of naming him. So she did not even dare to say, "My God," but "My Creator, have mercy on me!" And Saint Jerome writes that, thanks to such humility, she saw a glorious throne prepared for her in heaven.[3] Likewise in the life of Saint Margaret of Cortona we read that when our Lord visited her one day with greater tenderness and love, she exclaimed; "But, O Lord, how can this be? Have you forgotten what I was? How is it that you repay all my insults against you with so much delicate attention?" And God replied that when a soul loves him, and repents of having offended him, he forgets all her past offenses. As he said through Ezekiel, "But if the wicked turn away from all their sins...none of the transgressions that they have committed shall be remembered

against them" (Ezek 18:21–22). And in proof of this, he showed her a high throne, which he had prepared for her in heaven in the midst of the seraphim.[4] If only we could understand the value of humility! A single act of humility is worth more than all the riches in the world.

4 • Saint Teresa used to say, "Don't think that you have made progress in perfection until you consider yourself the worst of all, and unless you desire to be placed last."[5] And that is what the saint did,[6] as all the other saints have done. Saint Francis of Assisi,[7] Saint Mary Magdalen de Pazzi,[8] and the rest considered themselves the greatest sinners in the world, and were surprised that the earth bore them up, rather than opening beneath their feet; and they said so with sincere conviction. The Venerable Father John of Ávila, who had led a holy life from his youth, had a priest come to assist him on his deathbed. The priest said some quite sublime things to him, treating him as the great servant of God and great divine that he was. But Father Ávila told him: "Father, I beg you, pray for my soul, as one prays for the soul of a criminal condemned to death; for that is what I am."[9] This is the estimation that the saints have of themselves in life and death.

5 • We, too, must act this way, if we wish to be saved and keep ourselves in God's grace until death, putting all our trust in God alone. The proud rely on their own strength, and so they fall; but the humble, by trusting God alone, stand firm and never fall, even when they are assaulted by the most violent temptations. Their watchword is: "I can do all things through him who strengthens me" (Phil 4:13). The devil at one time tempts us to presumption, at another time to despair. When he tells us that we are in no danger of falling, then let us tremble

all the more; because if for one instant God were not to help us with his grace, we would be lost. When the devil tempts us to despair, then let us turn to God, and say with great confidence: "In you, O Lord, I seek refuge; do not let me ever be put to shame" (Ps 31:1). My God, in you I have placed all my hope; I hope I never have to see myself confounded nor bereft of your grace. We ought to make these acts of distrust in ourselves and trust in God up to the very last moments of our life, always begging God to grant us holy humility.

6 • But in order to be humble, it is not enough to have a lowly opinion of ourselves and to consider ourselves the wretches that we are. The person who is truly humble, says Thomas à Kempis, looks down on himself, and wishes to be looked down on by others.[10] That is what Jesus Christ recommends, following his example: "Learn from me, for I am gentle and humble in heart" (Mt 11:29). Those who call themselves the greatest sinners in the world, and then get angry when others despise them, plainly show that their humility is on their tongue, not in their heart. Saint Thomas Aquinas says that a person who resents being slighted may be sure that he is a long way from perfection, even if he were to work miracles.[11] The divine Mother sent Saint Ignatius Loyola to instruct Saint Mary Magdalen de Pazzi in humility; and here is the lesson that the saint gave her: "Humility is the enjoyment of whatever leads us to despise ourselves."[12] Note well, it is an enjoyment; if our senses are hurt by the scorn we receive, we must at least enjoy them with the spirit.

7 • And how could a soul who loves Jesus Christ, seeing how much God has endured, as he suffered in his Passion—"Then they spat in his face and struck him; and some slapped

him" (Mt 26:67)—how could that soul not love being scorned? That is why our Redeemer wanted his image exhibited on our altars, representing him not in glory, but nailed to the cross, that we might constantly have before our eyes the ignominy he suffered: a sight that made the saints rejoice to see themselves despised in this world. And such was the request that Saint John of the Cross made of Jesus Christ, when Jesus appeared to him with the cross upon his shoulder: "O Lord, let me suffer, and be despised for you!"[13] My Lord, as I see you thus despised for my love, I ask of you only to make me suffer and be despised for your love.

8 • Saint Francis de Sales says: "To put up with infamy is the touchstone of humility and of true virtue."[14] If a person claiming to be spiritual engages in prayer, frequent Communion, fasts, and mortification, and yet cannot put up with an affront or a biting word, what does that tell us? It shows that this person is a hollow reed, without humility and without virtue. And what can souls do who love Jesus Christ if they cannot endure a slight for the love of him who endured so many slights for them? Thomas à Kempis, in his golden book, *The Imitation of Christ,* writes as follows: "Since you have such a horror of being humiliated, that is a sign that you are not dead to the world, that you have no humility, and you do not keep God before your eyes. Those who do not have God before their eyes are disturbed by every word of blame that they hear."[15] You can't endure blows and wounds for God; endure at least a few words.

9 • Indeed, what surprise and scandal are caused by people who are frequent communicants yet who are quick to resent every scornful word! On the other hand, what fine

edification a soul gives who, when greeted with scorn, answers gently to conciliate the offensive individual; or perhaps makes no reply at all, nor complains to others, but maintains a placid expression, and shows no bitterness. Saint John Chrysostom says that the meek are beneficial not just to themselves but to others as well, because of the good example they give of gentleness in the face of contempt.[16]

On this topic Kempis mentions a number of areas in which we should practice humility. He writes: "What others say will get a hearing, and what you say will be disparaged. Others will ask for something and get it. You will ask and be refused. Others will be loudly praised by their colleagues, and you will be passed over in silence. This or that assignment will be conferred on others, while you will be judged as good for nothing. The Lord uses such trials to test his faithful servants, to see how they have learned to control themselves and stay calm. At times human nature will protest; but you will profit greatly if you bear it all in silence."[17]

10 • Saint Jane Frances de Chantal used to say, "When those who are truly humble receive a humiliation, they humble themselves even more."[18] Indeed, because those who are truly humble never think they have been humiliated as much as they deserve. Those who behave this way are called blessed by Jesus Christ. He does not call blessed people who are esteemed, honored, and praised as noble, learned, or powerful, but the ones who are spoken ill of by the world, who are persecuted and calumniated. For these—if only they bear it all with patience—has been prepared a great reward in paradise: "Blessed are you when people revile you and persecute you and utter all kinds of evil against you falsely on my account. Rejoice and be glad, for your reward is great in heaven" (Mt 5:11–12).

11 • The chief occasion for practicing humility is when we are rebuked for some fault by superiors or others. Some people are like hedgehogs: when no one touches them, they seem quite placid and gentle; but no sooner does a superior or a friend lay a hand on them, admonishing them about something they have done badly, than they suddenly become all prickles, and bitingly reply that it isn't true, or that they were right to act the way they did, or that such a correction is uncalled for. In a word, anyone who reproves them becomes their enemy; they behave like the people who accuse the surgeon for causing them pain while treating their wound. "He is angry with the doctor," writes Saint Bernard.[19] When holy and humble people are corrected, says Saint John Chrysostom, they grieve for the mistake they have made. By contrast, upon receiving correction proud people grieve too; but they grieve because their faults have been found out. And so they are troubled, they answer back, and are furious at the persons who correct them.[20] Here is the golden rule cited by Saint Philip Neri for those receiving corrections: "Anyone who would really become a saint must never excuse himself, even when the accusation is false."[21]

The one exception to this rule is when self-defense seems to be necessary to avoid scandal. Souls earn great rewards from God when they keep silent and do not make excuses even if wrongfully accused. Saint Teresa said: "Sometimes a soul makes more progress and acquires greater perfection by not offering excuses than by listening to ten sermons; because by not hiding behind excuses the soul begins to win freedom of spirit, and to stop caring whether people speak well or ill of her."[22]

Prayers of Love and Affection

Incarnate Word, I beg you, by the merits of your holy humility, which led you to embrace so many ignominies and insults for your love, free me from all pride and grant me a share of that humility. And how could I ever complain of any affront to myself, especially after I have so often deserved hell? My Jesus, by the merit of all the scorn you endured for me in your Passion, grant me the grace to live and die humbled on this earth, as you lived and died humbled for my sake. For your love I would willingly be despised and forsaken by everyone; but without you I can do nothing.

I love you, my sovereign good; I love you, beloved of my soul. I love you; and I hope—and this is my purpose—to suffer everything for you, insults, betrayals, persecutions, afflictions, dryness, and desolation, as long as you do not abandon me. My soul's only beloved, never again let me wander away from you.

Give me the desire to please you. Give me fervor in loving you. Give me peace of mind in suffering. Give me resignation in everything that goes against me.

Have mercy on me. I deserve nothing; but I hope for everything from you, who bought me with your blood.

And I hope for everything from you, my queen and mother Mary, the refuge of sinners.

X

"Love Is Not Arrogant": Those Who Love Jesus Christ Aspire to Nothing but Jesus Christ

1 • Those who love God do not go off seeking the esteem and love of others. Their only desire is to be cherished by God, who is the only object of their love. Saint Hilary writes that all honor received from the world is the business of the devil.[1] And so it is; for the enemy is dealing on behalf of hell when he fills souls with the desire for the esteem of others; because, in losing humility, these souls run the danger of plunging into every kind of evil. Saint James writes that as God opens his hands to pour out his grace upon the humble, so he closes them against the proud, whom he resists. "God opposes the proud, but gives grace to the humble" (Jas 4:6). "Opposes the proud" means that he does not even hear their prayers. And one of the acts of pride is surely aspiring to be honored by other people and growing conceited over honors received from them.

2 • A frightening example of this may be found in the story of the Franciscan Brother Justin, who had reached a high level of contemplation; but perhaps because—no, undoubtedly because—he cherished a desire to be esteemed by the world, here is what happened to him. One day Pope Eugenius IV

sent for him; and, having a high opinion of his sanctity, the pope showed him every honor, embraced him, and made him sit by his side. These favors went to Brother Justin's head. This prompted Saint John Capistrano to say to him, "O Brother Justin, you left an angel, and you returned a devil!" And in fact, with every passing day Brother Justin became more puffed up with pride; he demanded treatment befitting someone as important as himself. In the end he murdered one of the brothers with a knife; later he abandoned religious life and fled to the Kingdom of Naples, where he committed other atrocities and died in prison, an apostate to the end.[2]

That is why a great servant of God wisely said that when we hear or read of the fall of one of the "cedars of Lebanon," of a Solomon, a Tertullian, or a Hosius, who were all considered holy men, it is a sign that they were not given wholly to God, but inwardly nourished some spirit of pride and betrayed their office. So let us tremble, when we feel the stirrings of an ambition to be noticed and esteemed by the world. And when the world pays us some tribute, let us beware of becoming complacent about it, which might lead to our ruin.

3 • Let us especially be on our guard against the ambition to surpass others in honor. Saint Teresa said, "Where the quest for honor prevails, the spirit will never be."[3] Many persons profess to lead a spiritual life but are worshipers of their own self-esteem. They display certain apparent virtues, but what they really want is to be praised in all their undertakings; and if nobody else praises them, they will praise themselves. In a word, they strive to look better than others; and if ever they feel their self-esteem wounded, they lose their peace of mind, they stop going to Communion, they abandon all their devotions, and find no rest until they imagine they have recovered their

former standing. The true lovers of God do not act that way. Not only do they avoid saying anything in praise of themselves or indulging in complacency, but they are rather saddened by the praises that they receive from others. They are pleased to see themselves held in low repute among others.

4 • How true is the saying of Saint Francis of Assisi: "Whatever I am in the eyes of God is what I am."[4] What good is it to be considered great by the world, if we are vile and contemptible before God? And, on the contrary, what does it matter if we are despised by the world, as long as we are dear and acceptable to God? Saint Augustine writes that just as praise does not free us from the scourge of a bad conscience, neither does blame take away the merit of our good actions.[5] "What does it matter," says Saint Teresa, "if we be condemned and reviled by creatures, if in your sight we are great and blameless?"[6] The saints had no other desire than to live unknown to, and despised by, everyone. Saint Francis de Sales writes: "But what wrong do we suffer when people have a bad opinion of us, since we ought to have just such an opinion of ourselves? Perhaps we know that we are bad, and yet we expect that other people will take us for good."[7]

5 • How secure is the hidden life for those who wish to love Jesus Christ with all their hearts! Jesus Christ himself set us the example, by living hidden and scorned for thirty years in a workshop. And that is why, in order to shun human respect, the saints went and hid themselves in deserts and caves. Saint Vincent de Paul used to say that the pleasure of getting attention and the love of hearing people speak flatteringly of us and praise our conduct, when they say that we are succeeding and doing wonders, is an evil that, while it makes us forget God,

contaminates our most holy actions and proves to be the vice most damaging to our spiritual life.[8]

6 • Anyone, therefore, who wants to progress in the love of Jesus Christ must give the deathblow to the love of popularity. But how shall we inflict this blow? Here is how Saint Mary Magdalen de Pazzi instructs us: "The life of the appetite for popularity consists in being well regarded by everyone; consequently the death of popularity comes from keeping oneself hidden, so as not to be known to anyone. And until we learn to die in this manner, we shall never be true servants of God."[9]

7 • Thus to render ourselves pleasing in the sight of God, we must beware of the ambition to be conspicuous and pleasing in the eyes of the world. And we must avoid still more the ambition of dominating others. Saint Teresa said that sooner than have this accursed ambition make its way into the convent, she would rather see the whole place go up in smoke, and all the nuns with it. Hence she wished that if ever one of her sisters were found trying to become superior, she should be expelled from the community or at least kept locked up in her cell.[10] Saint Mary Magdalen de Pazzi said, "The honor of a spiritual person consists in being made the lowest of the low and in having a horror of being preferred over others."[11] The ambition of a soul that loves God should be to exceed all others in humility, as Saint Paul says, "In humility regard others as better than yourselves" (Phil 2:3). In a word, those who love God must aspire to nothing but God.

Chapter X

Prayers of Love and Affection

My Jesus, grant me the ambition of pleasing you, and make me forget all creatures, including myself. What good will it do me to be loved by the whole world, if I am not loved by you, the only love of my soul? My Jesus, you came into the world to win our hearts; if I cannot give you my heart, take it yourself, fill it up with your love, and never allow me to be separated from you again. In the past I have turned my back upon you; but now, seeing the wrong I have done, I regret it with all my heart, and there is no pain that afflicts me more than the memory of the many offenses that I have committed. But I am consoled by knowing that you are infinite goodness, that you do not disdain to love a sinner who loves you.

My beloved Redeemer, sweetest love of my soul, in the past I have slighted you; but now I love you more than my life itself. I offer you myself and all that is mine. I desire nothing but to love you, and to please you. That is my ambition; accept it and increase it, and destroy in me every desire for worldly goods. You are greatly worthy of being loved, and have greatly obliged me to love you.

Here I am, I wish to be entirely yours; and I want to suffer as much as you want me to, you who for love of me died in pain on the cross. You want me to be a saint; you can make me a saint; in you I put my trust.

And I also confide in your protection, O Mary, great Mother of God!

XI

"Love Does Not Insist on Its Own Way": Those Who Love Jesus Christ Seek to Detach Themselves From Every Created Thing

1 • Those who desire to love Jesus Christ with their whole heart must banish from their heart all that is not God, but is self-love. That is the meaning of the phrase, "does not insist on its own way." We are not to seek ourselves, but only what pleases God. And this is what the Lord demands of us all when he says: "You shall love the Lord your God with all your heart" (Mt 22:37).

To love God with all our heart two things are required: (1) to clear away the earth from it and (2) to fill it with holy love. Thus a heart in which any earthly affections remain can never belong wholly to God. Saint Philip Neri said that, as much love as we invest in other creatures, we take away just that much from God.[1] But how is the heart to be purged of the earth? With mortification and detachment from created things. Some souls complain that they seek God and do not find him. Let them listen to what Saint Teresa says: "Detach your heart from creatures, and seek God, and you will find him."[2]

2 • Some people are deceived because they wish to become saints, but after their own fashion. They want to love Jesus Christ, but in their own way, without giving up their diversions, their vanity of dress, their appetizing foods.

They love God, but if they do not succeed in obtaining such and such a position, they live restless lives. If their self-esteem is offended, they flare up; if they don't recover quickly from an illness, they lose all patience. They love God; but they won't let go of their attachment to riches, to worldly honors, to the vanity of being thought noble, wise, and better than others. Such individuals say their prayers and go to Communion; but because they bring with them hearts full of earth, they derive little profit from it. The Lord does not even speak to them, for he knows he would be wasting his words. He said just that to Saint Teresa one day: "I would speak to many souls, but the world makes so much noise in their ears that they cannot hear my voice. Oh, if only they would stand a little apart from the world!"[3]

Hence, people who are full of earthly affections cannot even hear the voice of God that is speaking to them. How unhappy are those who are attached to the sensible goods of this earth; they may easily become so blinded by them so that one day they abandon the love of Jesus Christ; and for fear of losing these transitory goods they may lose God, the infinite good, forever. Saint Teresa said: "It follows rightly that one who runs after lost goods should be lost himself."[4]

3 • Saint Augustine writes that Tiberius Caesar wanted the Roman senate to enroll Jesus Christ among their gods; but the senate refused to do so, on the ground that he was too proud a God, and wanted be worshiped all by himself without any companions.[5]

That is quite true: God wants us to adore and love him exclusively, not out of pride, but because he deserves it and also because of the love he bears us. Since he himself loves us so much, he wants all our love; and so he is jealous of anyone else's sharing the hearts that he wants all for himself. "Jesus is a jealous lover," says Saint Jerome.[6] That is why he doesn't want us fixing our affections on anything but himself. And whenever he sees that any created object has a hold on our hearts, he envies it, so to speak, as the apostle James says, because he will not endure rivals in love. He wants to be loved alone: "Or do you suppose that it is for nothing that the Scripture says, 'God yearns jealously for the spirit that he has made to dwell in us'?" (Jas 4:5). In the Song of Solomon, the Lord praises his spouse, saying: "A garden locked is my sister, my bride, a garden locked, a fountain sealed" (Song 4:12). He calls her "a garden locked," because souls wedded to him close their hearts to all earthly love in order to keep their love for Jesus Christ, and no one else.

Could it be that Jesus Christ doesn't deserve all our love? He deserves it only too well, both because of his own goodness and because of his love for us. The saints clearly understand this, which was why Saint Francis de Sales said: "If I knew that I had one fiber in my heart that did not belong to God, I would want to tear it out immediately."[7]

4 • David longed to have wings free from the snare of worldly affections in order to fly away and rest in God: "O that I had wings like a dove! I would fly away and be at rest" (Ps 55:6).

Many souls would like to see themselves released from every earthly trap to fly to God, and they would indeed soar to holiness, if they would detach themselves from everything in this world. But because they hold on to some little inordinate affection and will not force themselves to get rid of it, they remain forever languishing in their misery, without ever lifting a foot off the ground. Saint John of the Cross said: "Souls that remain with their affections attached to anything, however small, will, however many virtues they may possess, never arrive at divine union. For it matters little whether the bird be tied by a slender thread or a thick one; since, slight as it may be, so long as one does not break it, one remains tied down and unable to fly. Oh, how pitiful a thing it is to see certain souls, rich in spiritual exercises, in virtues and divine favors; yet, because they lack the courage to break with that little disordered affection, they cannot attain divine union, which only requires one strong and resolute surge to break the fatal thread! For, once souls are freed from all affection for creatures, God cannot but give himself fully to them."[8]

5 • Those who want God to be entirely theirs must give themselves entirely to God: "My beloved is mine," says the Spouse and I am his" (Song 2:16). My beloved has given himself entirely to me, and I have given myself entirely to him. Because of the love that he bears us, Jesus Christ wants all our love; and unless he has it all, he is never satisfied. This is what led Saint Teresa to write to the prioress at one of her convents: "Strive to train souls detached from every created thing, because they are being trained to be spouses of a king so jealous that he would have them forget even themselves."[9] Saint Mary Magdalen de Pazzi took a little book of devotion away from one of her novices, simply because she noticed that she was far too attached to it.[10] Many souls make mental prayer, visit the Blessed Sacrament, and receive holy Communion frequently; but still they make little or no progress in perfection, because

their hearts are attached to some earthly affection. And if they continue to live this way, not only will they always be wretched, but they run the risk of losing everything.

6 • We must, therefore, join David in begging almighty God to rid our heart of all earthly attachments: "Create in me a clean heart, O God" (Ps 51:10). Otherwise we can never be entirely his. He has made it very clear that those who do not renounce everything in this world cannot be his true disciples: "So therefore, none of you can become my disciple if you do not give up all your possessions" (Lk 14:33). For this reason whenever a young man came to join their company, the ancient Fathers of the desert used to ask this question: "Do you bring an empty heart, so that the Holy Spirit may fill it?"[11] Our Lord said the same thing to Saint Gertrude when she asked him what he wanted of her: "I want nothing else from you but a heart empty of creatures."[12] So we must say to God with a strong and resolute mind: Lord, I prefer you to everything, to health, to riches, to honors and dignities, to praise, to learning, to consolations, to hopes, to desires, and even to the very graces and gifts that I may receive from you. In short, I prefer you to every created good that is not you, O my God. Whatever gift you give me, O my God, nothing besides yourself is enough for me. I want you alone, and nothing more.

7 • When a heart is detached from every affection for created things, God's love immediately enters and fills it. Moreover, Saint Teresa said: "As soon as the occasions of sin are removed, the heart at once turns to love God."[13] Indeed, because the soul cannot live without loving, it must either love the Creator or creatures.

In short, we must abandon everything to gain everything. "*Totum pro toto*," says Thomas à Kempis, "Everything for everything."[14] As long as Saint Teresa cherished a certain affection, even though it was pure, for one of her relatives, she did not wholly belong to God. But later when she summoned up the courage and broke off the attachment, then she deserved to hear these words from Jesus: "Now, Teresa, you are all mine, and I am all yours."[15] One heart is just too small to love this God, who is so loving and so lovable that he deserves an infinite love. And would we divide that heart between creatures and God? The Venerable L. da Ponte felt ashamed to say to God: "O Lord, I love you above all things, above riches, honors, friends, relatives"; because it seemed that he was saying to God: "O Lord, I love you more than mud, than smoke, and the worms of the earth."[16]

8 • The prophet Jeremiah says: "The Lord is good to those who wait for him, to the soul that seeks him" (Lam 3:25). But he is speaking of a soul that seeks God alone. O happy loss! O happy gain! to lose worldly goods, which cannot satisfy the heart and quickly pass away, to obtain the sovereign and eternal good, which is God! We are told that one day a prince betook himself to a forest where a holy hermit lived. Seeing the hermit wandering through the wilderness, he asked him who he was and what was he doing. The hermit replied, "And you, my lord, what are you doing in this wilderness?" The prince said, "I am hunting animals." "And I," the hermit replied, "am hunting God." And so saying, he went off on his way.[17]

In the present life this must likewise be our only thought, our only purpose, to go searching for God, in order to love him, and for his will, in order to fulfill it, dismissing from our heart all creaturely affection. And whenever some worldly good presents itself to win over our love, let us have our answer ready: "I have contemned the kingdom of the world, and all the allurements of the present age, for the love of my Lord Jesus Christ."[18] And what are all the dignities and grandeurs of this world but smoke, mire, and vanity, which all disappear at death? Blessed are those who can say: "My Jesus, I have left all for your love; and you are my only love; you alone are enough for me."

9 • When the love of God takes full possession of souls, of their own accord—though always, of course, with the help of divine grace—these souls strive to divest themselves of every earthly thing that might prevent them from belonging completely to God. Saint Francis de Sales said that when a house catches fire, people throw all the furniture out the window,"[19] meaning that when a person gives himself entirely to God, without being urged on by preachers or confessors, that person spontaneously seeks to get rid of every earthly affection.

Father Segneri, Jr., said that divine love is a robber, who readily strips us of everything, so that we may own nothing but God.[20] A certain well-respected man renounced all his possessions and became poor for the love of Jesus Christ. When a friend asked him how he had been reduced to such a state of poverty, he pulled out of his pocket a little copy of the Gospels, and said: "Look, here is what stripped me of everything."[21]

The Holy Spirit says: "If one offered for love all the wealth of his house, it would be utterly scorned" (Song 8:7). And when souls bestow all their love on God, they despise everything—wealth, pleasures, dignities, lands, kingdoms—and want nothing but God. They each say and keep repeating: "My God, I want you alone, and nothing more." Saint Francis de Sales writes: "The pure love of God consumes everything that is not God, to convert all into itself; because everything done for the love of God is love."[22]

10 • The holy spouse says: "He brought me to the banqueting house, and his intention to me was love" (Song 2:4). This banqueting house (rendered as "wine cellar" in the Vulgate), writes Saint Teresa, "is divine love, which, when it takes possession of a soul, so inebriates it as to make it forget the whole created world."[23] A drunkard is, as it were, dead to his senses: the intoxicated neither sees nor hears nor speaks. And the same thing happens to the soul drunk with divine love. It no longer has any sense of the things of the world; the soul wants to think only of God, to speak only of God, and has no intention of doing anything but loving and pleasing God. In the Song of Solomon the Lord forbids anyone to awake his beloved, who is sleeping: "I adjure you...do not stir up or awaken love until it is ready" (Song 2:7). This blessed sleep, which is enjoyed by souls wedded to Jesus Christ, says Saint Basil, is nothing but "the complete oblivion of all things,"[24] a virtuous and voluntary forgetting of every created thing, in order to attend only to God, and to be able to say, as Saint Francis did, "My God and my all."[25] My God, what are riches and dignities and goods of the world? You are my everything and my every good. "*My God and my all*," writes Thomas à Kempis, "Oh, sweet word. My God, my everything. For those who understand, this says enough. And for those who love, it is sweet to say over and over again: My God and my all, my God and my all."[26]

11 • Therefore, to arrive at perfect union with God, one must be totally detached from creatures. And to get down to particulars, we must distance ourselves from inordinate affection for relatives. Jesus Christ says: "Whoever comes to me and does not hate father and mother, wife and children, brothers and sisters, yes, and even life itself, cannot be my disciple" (Lk 14:26). Why this hatred for relatives? Because with regard to spiritual profit, our first enemies are often our own kin: "And one's foes will be members of one's own household" (Mt 10:36). Saint Charles Borromeo said that when he went to his parents' house, he always came back spiritually chilled.[27] And when Father Antonio Mendoza was asked why he refused to stay in his parents' house, he replied, "Because I know from experience that nowhere do religious lose their devotion as much as in the house of their parents."[28]

12 • Saint Thomas Aquinas teaches that when it comes to the choice of a state of life, we are certainly not obliged to obey our parents.[29] Should a young man be called to the religious life, and meet resistance from his parents, he is bound to obey God, and not his parents, who, as Saint Thomas says, oppose our spiritual welfare for the sake of their own interests and private ends. "Friends of flesh and blood are oftentimes the enemies of our spiritual progress."[30] They would prefer, says Saint Bernard, to have their children damned rather than leave home.[31]

13 • And it is surprising, in this area, to see certain fathers and mothers who, even though they fear God, are, as it were, so dazzled by passion that they wear themselves out and leave no stone unturned to block the vocation of a child who wants to become a religious. Except in very rare cases those who do so cannot be excused from grievous sin.

But someone may say: Then if that youth doesn't become a religious, can't he be saved? Will everyone who remains in the world be damned? I answer: those whom God does not call to religion will be saved in the world by fulfilling the duties of their state. But those who are called and do not obey God may, indeed, be saved, but with difficulty; because they will lack those special helps that the Lord had prepared for them in religious life, and without which they will not reach salvation. The theologian Habert writes that those who do not obey their divine vocation remain in the Church like a member removed from where it belongs, and they have a great deal of difficulty in performing their duty and so in obtaining salvation.[32] Whence he concludes: "Although, absolutely speaking, they can be saved, yet they will enter on the way of salvation and lay hold of the means of salvation only with difficulty."[33]

14 • Father Granata compares the choice of a state of life to the mainspring in a watch:[34] if the mainspring gets broken, the whole watch is out of order. And so, with regard to our salvation, if we make the wrong choice of a state of life, our whole life will go wrong too. So many poor young men have lost their vocation because of their parents, and then have come to a bad end, while they themselves have been the ruin of their family. One youth lost his religious vocation at the prodding of his father; but later he came to hold his father in great revulsion; in fact he killed him with his own hand and was executed for the crime. Another young man, while living in a seminary, also received a call from God to leave the world. Neglecting his vocation, he first gave up the devout life he was leading, prayer, and Communion; then he abandoned himself to vice; and finally one night, as he was leaving the house of a loose woman, he was murdered by a rival. A number of priests hurried to the spot, but they found him already dead. And I could cite many other examples like these.

15 • But, to return to our subject, Saint Thomas advises those who are called to a more perfect life not to ask their parents' advice, because in this matter parents turn into enemies.[35]

And if children are not bound to take the advice of their parents on their vocation, they are still less obliged to wait for their permission, or even to ask for it, as long as they have reason to fear that it might be unjustly denied them, thereby impeding their vocation. Saint Thomas Aquinas, Saint Peter of Alcántara, Saint Francis Xavier, Saint Louis Bertrand, and many others, entered religion without even informing their parents about it.

16 • Furthermore, it must be observed that just as those who abandon their vocation to please their parents are in great danger of damnation, so on the other hand those who, without a call from God, enter the ecclesiastical state for fear of displeasing their parents are putting their eternal salvation at great risk. There are three signs that distinguish a true vocation to such a sublime state: knowledge, the purpose of attending only to God, and goodness of life. Speaking in particular about goodness, the Council of Trent ordered bishops to promote to Holy Orders only those who have already been proved to be leading a good life. And the Council prescribes the amount of time that must pass before conferring the various orders: "So that with age they may increase in merit and knowledge of the faith."[36]

17 • The reason for this is cited by Saint Thomas: with each holy order the ordinand moves closer to the most sublime ministry, that of serving Jesus Christ in the sacrament of the altar. Hence the saint adds that the holiness of the priest ought to surpass that of the religious.[37] Elsewhere he says that Holy Orders "require holiness in advance":[38] in other words the candidate should be holy before being ordained. And Saint Thomas shows that the difference between religious life and the priesthood consists in the fact that in religion one purifies one's self of one's vices, but to receive Holy Orders one must be already purged of them by leading a holy life.

18 • In my *Moral Theology*[39] I have shown that those who receive any Holy Orders without having shown proof of a good life cannot be excused from mortal sin, because they have ascended to this sublime state without a divine calling. No one can claim he has been called by God if he receives Holy Orders while still not yet free from habitual vice, especially against chastity. Hence Saint Anselm says: "Those who thrust themselves [into Holy Orders] and seek only their own glory are robbers of God's grace; instead of God's blessing they receive his curse."[40] As Bishop Abelly remarks, "Anyone who knowingly and without considering whether he had a divine vocation were to intrude himself into the priesthood, would undoubtedly expose himself to eternal perdition."[41] What I have written is not just the opinion of one theologian (Soto, Sanchez, Holzman, and others say the same); it is the common opinion based upon the teaching of Saint Thomas.

19 • Thus when the ordinand receives Holy Orders without having led a good life, not only does he himself commit a mortal sin, but so does the bishop who ordains him without the required evidence of the good life of the candidate. His confessor also sins gravely in giving absolution to a habitual sinner. And parents, too, commit a serious sin when, although they know the wicked conduct of their sons, strive to get them to take Holy Orders for their own personal goals of helping the family.

Jesus Christ instituted the ecclesiastical state not to help secular households, but to promote the glory of God and the salvation of souls. Some imagine the priesthood to be a lay employment or trade for the sake of accumulating honors or temporal goods, but they are wrong. Thus when parents come to disturb the bishop by asking him to ordain one of their sons who is ignorant or whose conduct has been bad, pleading that their family is poor, and that they don't know what to do, the bishop must say to them: "No, my son, the ecclesiastical state was not founded to help families out of poverty, but to promote the good of the Church." He should send them away without a further hearing; for such unworthy persons tend to be the ruination not only of their own souls, but of their families and towns.

20 • As for priests who live at home, if their parents would rather they apply themselves to advancing the family's income and honor instead of the tasks of their ministry, they should give the same answer that Jesus Christ gave his divine Mother: "Did you not know that I must be in my Father's house?" (Lk 2:49). They must reply: "I am a priest; my duty is not to make money and seek honors, nor to manage the house, but to live in seclusion, to pray, to study, and to work for the salvation of souls." Should there be a specific need to help one's family, one ought to do so as far as possible without neglecting one's principal duty, which is to attend to the sanctification of oneself and of others.

21 • Moreover, anyone who wishes to belong wholly to God must be detached from human respect. Oh, how many people does this accursed need for approval drive far from God, and even cause them to lose him forever! For example, if they hear talk about their failings, they will do anything to justify themselves, and to convince others that it is all lies and calumny. If they do some good deed, they will do anything to let everyone know about it. They would like the whole world to know it—and to praise them. The saints behave differently: they would prefer that the whole world knew their faults, so that people would consider them the wretches that they take themselves to be. And, on the contrary, in performing any act of virtue, they want only God to know about it; since God is the only one they wish to please. That is why they love the hidden life so much, mindful of the teaching of Jesus Christ, who said: "But when you give alms, do not let your left hand know what your right hand is doing" (Mt 6:3). And in Matthew 6:6: "But whenever you pray, go into your room and shut the door and pray to your Father who is in secret."

22 • But above all, we must have detachment from ourselves, that is, from our own will.

Those who conquer themselves find it easy to conquer all their other repugnances. "Conquer yourself"[42] was the maxim which Saint Francis Xavier urged on everyone. And Jesus Christ said: "If any want to become my followers, let them deny themselves" (Mt 16:24). Here is all that we need do to become saints: deny ourselves and not follow our own will: "Do not follow your base desires, but restrain your appetites" (Sir 18:30). The greatest gift, said Saint Francis of Assisi, that we can receive from God is to conquer ourselves by denying our own will.[43] Saint Bernard writes that if everyone would resist self-will, no one would ever be damned: "Let self-will cease, and there will be no hell."[44] The same saint writes that self-will makes even our good deeds turn bad.[45] If, for example, a penitent wishes to do some mortification—fast or use the discipline—against the will of his or her spiritual father, this act of penance, prompted by self-will, becomes sinful.

Unhappy are those who live enslaved to their own self-will; for they will yearn for many things, but they will not be able to obtain them. On the contrary, they will refuse to suffer many things they find distasteful, and they will be forced to endure them. "Those conflicts and disputes among you, where do they come from? Do they not come from your cravings that are at war within you? You want something and do not have it" (Jas 4:1–2).

The first war arises from the appetite for sensual delights. Let us remove the occasion, let us mortify the eyes, let us commend ourselves to God; and the war will be over. The second war arises from greed for wealth: let us strive to love poverty, and the war will be over. The third war comes from the ambition for honors; let us love humility and the hidden life, and the war will be over. The fourth war, the most harmful of all, comes from self-will: let us resign ourselves to all things that happen by the will of God, and the war will be over. Saint Bernard tells us that whenever we see a person troubled, the origin of his trouble is his inability to satisfy his self-will.[46] The Lord once complained of this to Saint Mary Magdalen de Pazzi: "Certain souls want my spirit, but only as it pleases them; and so they become incapable of receiving it."[47]

23 • We must therefore love God as it pleases God, not as it pleases us. God wants the soul stripped of everything, in order to unite her to himself and to fill her up with his divine love. Saint Teresa writes: "The prayer of union strikes me as dying, almost completely, to all the things of this world, so as to enjoy God alone. One thing for sure is that the more we empty ourselves of creatures, by detaching ourselves from them for the love of God, the more he will fill us with himself, and the more we will be united with him."[48] Many spiritual persons would like to achieve union with God; but they shy away from the adversities that God sends them. They shy away from the infirmities that afflict them, from the poverty that they suffer, from the affronts they receive. But without resignation they will never come to perfect union with God. Let us hear what Saint Catherine of Genoa said: "To arrive at union with God, we must have the adversities that God sends us. He uses them to consume all our evil impulses, both within and without. And hence we greatly need all the contempt, sickness, deprivations, temptations, and other trials, so that we can do battle and win, so that our evil impulses may be extinguished and we may no longer feel them. Indeed until adversities no longer seem bitter to us but sweet for God's sake, we shall never arrive at divine union.[49]

24 • Let me add here the teaching of Saint John of the Cross. The saint says that for perfect union, "Total mortification of the senses and of the appetites is necessary. As for the senses, every single pleasure that presents itself to them, for any other purpose but the glory of God, should be rejected at once for the love of Jesus Christ. If, for example, one feels the urge to see or hear things that do not chiefly lead to God, then refrain from them. Then as for the appetites, we should always make an effort to choose the worst, the most disagreeable, or the poorest, without desiring anything except to suffer and be despised."[50]

In a word, those who truly love Jesus Christ lose all affection for worldly goods, and seek to strip themselves of everything, to be one with Jesus Christ alone. All their desires point to

Jesus; they are always thinking of Jesus and sighing for him; and in every place, at every time, on every occasion, they seek only to please Jesus. But to reach this point we must constantly aim to empty our hearts of all affection for anything but God.

I ask: what does it mean for the soul to give itself wholly to God? It means, first, to flee from anything that displeases God and to do what pleases him; second, it means to accept without reserve all that comes from his hands, however hard or unpleasant; and third, it means to prefer in all things the will of God to our own wishes: that is what it means to belong completely to God.

Prayers of Love and Affection

My God and my all, I feel that, despite all my ingratitude and negligence in serving you, you continue to call me to your love. Here I am, I no longer want to resist. I want to abandon everything so as to be wholly yours. I no longer wish to live for myself. Your claim to my love is too strong. My soul has fallen in love with you, my Jesus; it sighs after you. And how can I love anything else, after seeing you die in pain on a cross in order to save me? How could I look upon you dead and consumed with suffering, and not love you with all my heart? Yes, I love you, my dear Redeemer; I love you with all my soul; and I desire nothing except to love you in this life and for all eternity.

I ask you my love, my hope, my fortress and consolation, to give me the strength to be faithful to you. Give me light, and let me know what I should detach myself from. And give me strength, because I want to obey you in everything.

Love of my soul, I offer and give myself to you completely, to satisfy your desire to unite yourself to me, that I may be wholly united to you, my God and my all. Come, my Jesus, and take possession of my whole self, and draw to yourself all my thoughts and all my affections.

I renounce all my appetites, all my consolations, and all created things: you alone are enough for me. Give me the grace to think of nothing but you, to desire nothing but you, to seek nothing but you, my beloved and my only good!

O Mary, Mother of God, beg for me the grace of holy perseverance.

XII

"Love Is Not Irritable": Those Who Love Jesus Christ Never Get Angry With Their Neighbor

1 • The virtue not to become angry when things go against us derives from meekness. We have already said a number of things in the preceding chapters about the behavior proper to meekness and gentleness; but, since this is a virtue that must be continuously practiced by those who live in society, we shall make a few more points here in greater detail and a more practical vein.

2 • Humility and meekness were virtues dear to Jesus Christ, which is why he told his disciples, "Learn from me; for I am gentle and humble in heart" (Mt 11:29). Our Redeemer was called "the Lamb of God" (Jn 1:29), both because of the sacrifice that he was destined to offer of himself on the cross to atone for our sins, and because of the meekness that he showed throughout his life, and especially at the time of his Passion. When in the house of Caiphas, he received a blow from an officer, who at the same time treated him as a rash and reckless person ("Is that how you answer the high priest?" [Jn 18:22]), Jesus said only, "If I have spoken wrongly, testify to the wrong. But if I have spoken rightly, why do you strike me?"

(Jn 18:23). He continued to display the same meekness until death. While he hung on the cross and everyone mocked and blasphemed him, he did nothing but beg the Eternal Father to forgive them: "Father, forgive them; for they do not know what they are doing" (Lk 23:34).

3 • How very dear to Jesus Christ are those meek hearts who, when they suffer affronts, derision, calumnies, persecutions, and even beatings and wounds, do not grow angry at those who insult or strike them: "The prayer of the humble and the meek has always pleased you" (Jdt 9:16; Vulgate). God is always pleased with the prayers of the meek; that is to say, their prayers are always heard. The meek are promised paradise in a special way: "Blessed are the meek, for they shall inherit the earth" (Mt 5:5). Father Baltasar Álvarez said that heaven is the homeland of the despised, the persecuted, and the downtrodden; because the possession of that eternal kingdom has been reserved for them, and not for the proud, who are honored and esteemed by the world.[1] David declares that the meek will not only inherit eternal happiness, but will enjoy great peace even in this life: "The meek shall inherit the land, and delight themselves in abundant prosperity" (Ps 37:11).

The saints bear no malice against those who mistreat them, but love them all the more; and the Lord, as a reward for their patience, heightens their inner peace. Saint Teresa said: "I seem to have poured out a new love onto those who spoke ill of me."[2] This led the Sacred Roman Rota to say of the saint that insults provided her with an opportunity to love even more the person who had insulted her.[3] Such meekness is within the reach only of those endowed with great humility and a low opinion of themselves, so that they feel they deserve every kind of scorn. And hence we see, on the other hand, that the proud are always angry and vindictive, because they have a high opinion of themselves, and consider themselves worthy of all honor.

4 • "Blessed are the dead who from now on die in the Lord" (Rev 14:13). We have to die in the Lord to be blessed, and to begin to enjoy that blessedness even in this life: this means, the blessedness that can be had before entering heaven, which is certainly much less than the happiness of heaven, yet far exceeds all the pleasures of sense in this world: "And the peace of God, which passes all understanding, will guard your hearts and your minds in Christ Jesus" (Phil 4:7). So wrote the apostle Paul to his disciples. But to achieve this peace, even amid insults and affronts, we must be dead in the Lord.

A dead person, however mistreated and trampled on by others, does not mind it at all. Similarly, the meek, like corpses that no longer see or feel, must endure all the disdain heaped on them. Those who love Jesus Christ from the heart will easily attain this; because, as they are fully conformed to his will in all things, they accept with the same composure and peace of mind both prosperity and adversity, consolation and affliction, affronts and favors. That is what the apostle Paul did; and hence he says: "I am overjoyed in all our affliction" (2 Cor 7:4).

Happy are those who reach this level of virtue! They enjoy continuous peace, which is the best of all things in this world. Saint Francis de Sales said: "What is the whole world worth in comparison with peace of heart?"[4] In truth, what good are all the riches and honors of the world to people who live in restlessness, and whose heart is not at peace?

5 • In short, to remain forever united to Jesus Christ, we must do everything with serenity, untroubled by any adversity we may encounter. "The LORD was not in the earthquake" (1 Kings 19:11). The Lord does not dwell in troubled hearts.

Let us listen to the beautiful lessons given on this subject by that master of meekness Saint Francis de Sales: "Never get angry, never open the door to anger under any pretext; because, once it has entered us, we can no longer expel or moderate it when we wish. So the remedies against anger are: (1) reject it immediately, by distracting your mind, and not saying a word; (2) imitate the apostles when they saw the storm on the Sea of Galilee; turn to God, who brings peace to the heart; (3) if you see that, because of your weakness, anger has already gotten a foothold in your spirit, force yourself to calm down and then try to act humbly and gently toward the person with whom you are irritated. But all this must be done with delicacy and without violence, for it is very important not to rub salt into the wounds."[5] And apropos of self-control, the saint said that he himself had to struggle during his life to overcome his two predominant passions, namely, anger and love. To subdue the passion of anger, he confessed, had cost him twenty-two years of hard effort. As for the passion of love, he had striven to change its object, by leaving creatures behind and shifting all his affections to God.[6] And in this way the saint acquired an inner peace so great that it showed even on the outside; because he almost always had a serene expression and a smile on his face.[7]

6 • "Those conflicts…among you, where do they come from? Do they not come from your cravings that are at war within you?" (Jas 4:1). When we feel shaken by anger because

of some confrontation, we think we will find relief and peace by venting that anger in actions or at least in words. But we are wrong; because after letting off steam, we find we are much more upset than before. Anyone who wishes to have continuous peace of mind must beware of ever yielding to ill-humor. And whenever we feel trapped in a bad mood, we should try to dispel it immediately and not linger over it, distracting ourselves by reading a book, by singing a snatch of a hymn, or by discussing some pleasant topic with a friend. The Holy Spirit says: "Anger lodges in the bosom of fools" (Eccl 7:9). Anger finds a long-lasting place in the heart of fools, who have little love for Jesus Christ; but if it ever stealthily enters the heart of the lovers of Jesus Christ, it is quickly driven out and does not make its dwelling there. Souls that love the Redeemer from their hearts never feel in bad spirits, because, as they want only what God wants, they always have everything they wish, and so always find themselves tranquil and composed. God's will brings them serenity in every misfortune; and thus they behave meekly with one and all. But we cannot acquire this meekness without a great love for Jesus Christ. In fact, we are never so meek and gentle toward others as when we feel greater tenderness toward Jesus Christ.

7 • But since we cannot always experience this tenderness, we must prepare ourselves in mental prayer to suffer the blows that may befall us. That is what the saints did; so they were ready to receive with patience and meekness the insults, the blows, and the wounds. When we meet with abuse from our neighbor, unless we have often prepared ourselves in advance, we shall have a hard time discerning what to do to prevent anger from overcoming us. In the heat of the moment, it will seem reasonable for us to meet with the audacity of the person mistreating us; but Saint John Chrysostom says that it is wrong to try to put out the fire burning in the mind of our neighbor with the fire of an angry reply. That will only feed the flames: "Fire," he writes, "cannot be extinguished by fire."[8]

Some may say that it is unreasonable to be courteous and gentle with a reckless person who insults you for no reason at all. But Saint Francis de Sales replies: "We must practice meekness, not only with reason, but against reason."[9]

8 • So when attacked, we must try to answer with a few kind words; that is the way to put out the fire: "A soft answer turns away wrath" (Prov 15:1). But when the mind is troubled, the best solution will be to keep silent. Saint Bernard writes: "The eye troubled by anger does not see what is right."[10] When the eye is dimmed by indignation, it no longer can tell what is just from what is unjust; passion is like a veil drawn over the eyes, so that we cannot distinguish right from wrong. So we must do what Saint Francis de Sales did: "I have made a pact with my tongue," he wrote, "not to speak when my heart is disturbed."[11]

9 • But sometimes it does seem necessary to rebuke an insolent person with harsh words. David said: "When you are angry, do not sin" (Ps 4:4). But here is the point: in theory there are times when it seems appropriate to respond sharply to some people, to make them mend their ways. But in practice it is very difficult to do this without incurring some fault; so the sure way is always to admonish or answer them gently, and to be careful never to take offense. Saint Francis de Sales said: "I have never resented something without afterwards regretting it."[12] And when we clash with someone and still feel heated up about it, the safest way, as I said before, is to keep silence

and put off the reply or admonition until a more opportune moment, when the heart has cooled down.

10 • We ought to practice this meekness especially when we are corrected by our superiors or friends. Saint Francis de Sales writes: "To accept reprimands gratefully shows that we love the virtues contrary to the faults for which we have been reprimanded; and hence this is a great sign that we are making progress toward perfection."[13]

In addition, we must show meekness toward ourselves. The devil makes us think that it is laudable to be angry with ourselves when we commit some fault. But it is no such thing: the enemy is trying to keep us in a state of restlessness so that we will be unfit to do any good. Saint Francis de Sales said: "You can be sure that all thoughts which cause disquiet are not from God, who is the Prince of Peace, but come either from the devil, our self-love or from the high opinion we have of ourselves. These are the three sources from which all our troubles arise. Therefore, when any disquieting thoughts come to us, we must immediately reject and despise them."[14]

11 • Furthermore, meekness is absolutely necessary when we have to reprove others. Overzealous corrections often do more harm than good, especially when the person to be corrected is himself troubled. In that case we must hold back from correcting that person and wait until his boiling anger has subsided. And hence we should refrain from correcting others when we are in a bad mood; because then our admonition will always have a bitter taste to it. And the guilty parties, when they hear themselves rebuked in such a way, will disregard the admonitions as an ill-tempered outburst. This holds true with regard to the good of our neighbor. As far as our own advantage goes, let us show how we love Jesus Christ by peacefully and cheerfully enduring mistreatment, insults, and scorn.

Prayers of Love and Affection

My despised Jesus, you are the love and joy of my soul. By your example you have made being despised so pleasant to those who love you. From this day forward, I promise you to submit to every affront for the love of you, who for love of me were scorned on this earth by human beings. Give me strength to keep this promise. Make me know and do whatever you want from me.

My God and my all, I wish to seek no other good but you, who are infinite goodness. You who take such care of my interests, make me have no other care except to please you. Grant that all my thoughts may always be employed in fleeing anything that offends you, and in finding a way to please you in everything. Drive far from me every occasion that distracts me from your love. I strip myself of my freedom and consecrate it entirely to your good pleasure.

I love you, infinite goodness. I love you, my delight. My Word Incarnate, I love you more than myself. Have mercy on me, and heal all the wounds in my soul from its offenses against you. I abandon myself completely into your arms, my Jesus; I want to be yours completely; I want to suffer everything for your love; and I want nothing from you but yourself.

Holy Virgin and my Mother Mary, I love you, and I trust in you; help me with your powerful intercession.

XIII

"Love Is Not Resentful": It Does Not Rejoice at Wrongs, but Rejoices in the Right; Those Who Love Jesus Christ Want Nothing Except What Jesus Christ Wants

1 • Love and truth always go together. Since love knows that God is the one true good, it detests iniquity, which is opposed to God's will, and takes pleasure only in what God wills. Hence souls that love God do not care what people say about them, and seek only to do what pleases God. The Blessed Henry Suso said: "The ones who are on truly good terms with God are those who strive to fulfill the truth, and otherwise pay no heed to how they are treated or thought of by others."[1]

2 • We have already pointed out that all the holiness and perfection of a soul consists in denying oneself and in following the will of God; but here the point is even more relevant.

If we want to become saints, all our efforts must be aimed at never following our own will, but the will of God. The essence of all God's commands and counsels is to do and suffer what God wishes and how he wishes. Let us, therefore, beg the Lord to grant us a holy freedom of spirit that leads us to embrace whatever is pleasing to Jesus Christ, regardless of any repugnance caused by self-love or human respect. The love of

Jesus Christ puts his lovers into a state of total indifference: everything is the same to them, whether bitter or sweet. They want nothing that pleases themselves, only what is pleasing to God. With the same peace of mind they busy themselves in things great and small, pleasant and unpleasant; it is enough for them to please God.

3 • Saint Augustine says: "Love, and do what you want."[2] Those who really love God seek nothing but his pleasure; and in this they find all their contentment. Saint Teresa says: "Those who seek only the satisfaction of the one they love are satisfied by everything that pleases him. When love is perfect it has the strength to make a person forget all personal interests and pleasures, and focus all thoughts on pleasing the beloved, while trying to honor, and make others honor, the beloved. Lord, all our troubles come from not keeping our eyes fixed on you! If we had no other goal but moving ahead, we would quickly reach it. But we stumble and fall a thousand times, and we lose our way, for want of keeping a sharp eye out for the right path."[3] Here is what must be the sole aim of all our thoughts, actions, desires, and prayers: God's pleasure. And this has to be our path to perfection, to stick close to the will of God.

4 • Scripture says, "You shall love the Lord your God with all your heart" (Mt 22:37). The souls who love Jesus Christ with all their hearts are those who say to him with the apostle: "What am I to do, Lord?" (Acts 22:10). Lord, let me know what you want from me; for I wish to do it all. And we should realize that when we want what God wants, we want what is best for ourselves; because God surely wishes only the best for us. Saint Vincent de Paul said: "Conformity with the will of God is the Christian's treasure and the remedy for all

evils, because it contains abnegation of self, union with God, and all the virtues."[4] Here, then, is where all perfection lies: "What shall I do, Lord?" Jesus Christ promises us, "Not a hair of your head will perish" (Lk 21:18). This means that the Lord will repay us for every good thought that we have of pleasing him and for every tribulation patiently embraced by conforming to his holy will. Saint Teresa said, "The Lord never sends any distress, without rewarding us with some favor, so long as we accept it with resignation."[5]

5 • But our conformity to God's will must be entire, unreserved, and constant; we cannot go back on our word. This is the height of perfection; and this, I repeat, must be the goal of all our works, all our desires, and all our prayers. Some souls given to prayer, upon reading of the ecstasies and raptures of Saint Teresa, Saint Philip Neri, and other saints, dream of reaching this sort of supernatural union. Such longings must be dismissed, because they run counter to humility. If we wish to become saints, we must desire true union with God, which is to unite our will entirely to his. Saint Teresa writes: "Those who believe that union with God consists in ecstasies, raptures, and enjoyment of him are deceiving themselves. It consists in nothing more or less than in subjecting our will to the will of God. This subjection is perfect when our will is detached from everything and united only with God's, so that its every movement is what God alone wills. This is the true and essential union that I have always desired, and constantly beg of the Lord."[6] And then she adds: "Oh, how many of us say this; and we seem to want nothing else. But, wretches that we are, how few of us achieve it!"[7] And that is the truth: many of us say, "Lord! I give you all my will; I want nothing but what you want." But when adversity comes, we don't know how to yield

calmly to God's will. That is why we complain about having misfortune in the world, insisting that everything bad happens to us; and that we lead an unhappy life.

6 • If we were at one with God's will in all our adversities, we should surely become saints and be the happiest people in the world. Thus we must concentrate all our efforts on keeping our will united to the will of God in all that befalls us, whether pleasant or unpleasant.

The Holy Spirit warns us, "Do not winnow in with every wind" (Sir 5:9). Some people resemble weather vanes, turning whichever way the wind blows. If the wind favors their desires, we see them cheerful and meek; but if the wind is contrary, and things don't go as they would like, we see them sad and impatient. That is why they do not become saints and why their lives are unhappy, because in this life we always have more adversity than prosperity. Saint Dorotheus said that receiving all things, however they turn out, from the hands of God is a great way to maintain our peace of mind and tranquillity of heart. And for this reason, the saint tells us, the ancient Fathers of the desert were never seen angry or melancholy, because they gladly accepted whatever happened to them, as a gift from the hands of God.[8]

Happy are those who live wholly united and abandoned to God's will! They are neither puffed up by success nor downcast by failure; for they know that both come from the same hand of God. The will of God is the only thing that governs their will, and so they do only what God wants, and want only what God does. They do not undertake to do many things, just to accomplish perfectly what they understand to be God's good pleasure. Accordingly, they prefer the slightest obligations of their calling to the greatest and most glorious actions, because in the latter self-love may play a large part, whereas in the former the will of God is surely to be found.

7 • Thus we shall be blessed when we receive from God all the things he sends us in perfect conformity to his divine will, regardless of whether they suit our inclinations. Saint Jane Frances de Chantal asked: "When shall we come to enjoy the will of God in every event that happens to us, without regard to anything but God's good pleasure, which surely distributes both prosperity and adversity with equal love and looks out for our best interests? When shall we throw ourselves unreservedly into the arms of our most loving heavenly Father, leaving to him the care of our persons and our affairs, and reserving nothing for ourselves but the desire of pleasing God?"[9]

The friends of Saint Vincent de Paul used to say of him while he was still alive: "Monsieur Vincent is always Vincent."[10] They meant that no matter how things were going, the saint was always to be seen with the same serene expression and was always self-possessed, because, living in a state of complete surrender of himself to God, he feared nothing and wanted nothing except what was pleasing to God. Saint Teresa said: "This holy abandonment gives rise to the splendid freedom of spirit enjoyed by the perfect, in which may be found all the happiness one can desire in this life, since they neither fear nor wish nor yearn for the things of this world, because they already have everything."[11]

8 • On the other hand, many people devise a form of holiness to suit their own natural bent. The melancholy man exalts the life of a hermit; the busybody is all for preaching and reconciling enemies; harsh personalities seek out penance and mortifications; others who are naturally generous prize

almsgiving; still others like to visit sanctuaries, and therein lies all their holiness. External works arise out of love for Jesus Christ; but true love itself consists in total adhesion to the will of God and, consequently, in denying ourselves and choosing what is most pleasing to God, simply because he deserves it.

9 • Others wish to serve God—but only in a certain post, in a certain place, with certain companions, and under certain circumstances. Otherwise they either abandon their work or else do it grudgingly. Such people are not free in spirit, but slaves of self-love; and for that reason they earn little merit even for what they do. Instead, they live in perpetual disquiet, because their attachment to their own will makes the yoke of Jesus Christ weigh heavily on them.

The true lovers of Jesus Christ love only what pleases him and only because it pleases him; when, where, and how it pleases him; whether he chooses to employ them in places of honor or in mean and lowly tasks; in a life of celebrity in the world, or in a life hidden and neglected. This is the meaning of the pure love of Jesus Christ; and in this we must struggle against the appetites of self-love, which would have us busied only in works that bring us glory or personal satisfaction. And what does it profit us to be the most honored, the richest, or the greatest person in this world, without the will of God? The Blessed Henry Suso said, "I would rather be a vile insect crawling on the ground by the will of God, than a seraph in heaven by my own will."[12]

10 • Jesus Christ says: "On that day many will say to me, 'Lord, Lord, did we not prophesy in your name, and cast out demons in your name, and do many deeds of power in your name?'" (Mt 7:22). But the Lord will answer them: "I never knew you; go away from me, you evildoers" (Mt 7:23). Go away; I have never acknowledged you as my disciples, because you preferred to follow your own temperament rather than my will. This applies especially to those priests who toil for the salvation and perfection of others, while they themselves go on living in the swamp of their imperfections.

Perfection consists: (1) in true contempt of oneself; (2) in thorough mortification of our own appetites; and (3) in perfect conformity to the will of God. Anyone who lacks one of these virtues has strayed from the path of perfection. That is why a great servant of God once said that in our actions it was better to propose as our only aim the will of God; because in doing the will of God, we also procure his glory; whereas in aiming at the glory of God, we often deceive ourselves by doing our own will under the pretext of glorifying God. Saint Francis de Sales writes: "There are many who say to the Lord: I give myself to you completely and without reserve; but there are few who embrace this surrender in practice, which calls for a certain indifference in accepting all sorts of events, as determined by the order of divine Providence, afflictions as well as consolations, disparagement and disgrace as well as honor and glory."[13]

11 • Thus it is in suffering and in welcoming things that please us and thwart our self-love that we find out who are the true lovers of Jesus Christ. Thomas à Kempis says that no one deserves to be called a lover who is not ready to endure all things for the beloved, and to follow the will of the beloved in all things.[14] On the contrary, Father Baltasar Álvarez said that anyone who, when in distress, peacefully resigns himself to God's will "travels to God posthaste."[15] And holy Mother Teresa said: "What greater gain could we get than to have some proof that we are pleasing God?"[16] To this I add that we can have no more certain proof of pleasing God than by peacefully embracing the crosses that God sends us. The Lord is pleased when we thank him for the blessings he gives us on earth, but, as Venerable John of Ávila says, "one 'Blessed be God' in adversity is worth more than six thousand acts of thanksgiving in prosperity."[17]

12 • Here it should be observed that not only must we receive with resignation the adversity that comes directly from God, for example, sickness, lack of talent, or accidental losses, but also the sort of adversity that comes indirectly from God and directly from our own fellows, such as persecutions, thefts, or insults; because in truth they all come from God. One day David was showered with abuse by one of his vassals named Shimei, who not only insulted him, but even threw stones at him. Someone called for cutting off the head of the offender, but David replied: "Let him alone, and let him curse; for the LORD has bidden him" (2 Sam 16:11). In other words, God is making use of him to chastise me for my sins, and so he permits him to insult me in this way.

13 • Hence Saint Mary Magdalen de Pazzi said that all our prayers should have no other goal than to obtain from God the grace to follow his holy will in all things.[18] Some souls, greedy for spiritual pleasures in prayer, go off in search of sweet and tender feelings for their delectation. But brave souls with an honest desire to belong wholly to God ask him only for light to understand his will and for strength to carry it out perfectly.

To achieve purity of love our will must submit itself completely to the will of God: "Never think," said Saint Francis de Sales, "that you have arrived at the purity you ought to have, as long as your will has not cheerfully submitted, even in the most repulsive things, to the will of God."[19] Because, as Saint Teresa says, "The gift of our will to God leads him to unite himself to our lowliness."[20] But there is no way to obtain this except through meditation and constant prayer to his divine Majesty, as well as a sincere desire to belong wholly and unreservedly to Jesus Christ.

14 • Most lovable Heart of my divine Savior, O Heart in love with humankind, since you love us so tenderly, O Heart worthy of ruling and possessing all our hearts, if only I could make everyone understand the love you bear them, and your exquisite touches with those who love you without reserve. My Jesus, my love, please accept the offering and sacrifice that I make to you today of my entire will. Let me know what you want from me; for I wish to do everything with the help of your grace.

Obedience

15 • But what is the surest way to know and ascertain in our actions what God wants from us? There is no surer way than to practice obedience to our superiors or directors. Saint Vincent de Paul said: "The will of God is best carried out by obeying our superiors."[21] The Holy Spirit says: "Much better is obedience, than the victims of fools, who know not what evil they do" (Eccl 4:17; Vulgate). God is more pleased when we sacrifice our own will by subjecting it to obedience than with any other sacrifice we can offer him; because in almsgiving, fasts, mortification, and the like, we give God what belongs to us, but in giving him our will we give him ourselves. When we give him our goods or our mortifications, we give him part; but when we give him our will, we give him everything. So that when we say to God, "Lord, let me know by means of obedience what you want from me, for I want to do everything," we have nothing more to offer him.

16 • Thus all those who are dedicated to obedience must detach themselves completely from their own thinking. "Each one of us," says Saint Francis de Sales, "has his own opinions; but that is no obstacle to virtue. What is an obstacle to virtue is the attachment to our opinions."[22] Unfortunately this attachment is the hardest thing to part with; and hence there are so few souls who give themselves completely to God, because few make a thorough submission to obedience. Some people are so attached to their own opinion that, upon being told to do something, even though it be to their liking, the mere fact that they have to do it out of obedience makes them lose any wish to obey; for they find no pleasure except in doing what their own will dictates. But that is not how the saints behave; they find peace only in doing things that obedience imposes upon them. Once on a recreation day, Saint Jane de Chantal told her daughters that they might spend the time any way they liked. When evening came, they all went to her and urgently begged her not to grant them such a permission again; for they had never spent such a wearisome day as the one on which they had been set free from obedience.

17 • It is a delusion to think that any other work can be better than what obedience imposes on us. Saint Francis de Sales says: "To abandon a post assigned to us by obedience in order to unite ourselves to God by prayer, reading, or recollection, would be to withdraw from God to unite ourselves to our own self-love."[23] Saint Teresa adds that those who do any task, even a spiritual one, that is contrary to obedience, are surely working at the instigation of the devil, and not by divine inspiration, as they perhaps flatter themselves. "This is because," the saint says, "God's inspirations always go hand in hand with obedience.[24] Hence she writes elsewhere, "God wants nothing more from a soul that is determined to love him than obedience.[25] A work done out of obedience," says Father Rodriguez, "is worth more than any other that we can imagine. Picking up a straw from the ground out of obedience is worth more than choosing on our own to say a long prayer or to whip ourselves till the blood flows."[26] For this reason Saint Mary Magdalen de Pazzi said that she preferred to be engaged in some task assigned her by obedience than in prayer, "because," she said, "in obedience I am sure of doing the will of God, but in any other exercise I am by no means so certain."[27] All the spiritual masters tell us that it is better to abandon any devout exercise out of obedience than to continue doing it apart from obedience. The Blessed Virgin Mary revealed to Saint Bridget that those who give up an act of mortification out of obedience reap a double profit, since they have already gained the merit of the mortification by their willingness to do it, and they gain the merit of obedience by forgoing it.[28] One day the famous Father Francis Arias went to see his dear friend, the Venerable Father John of Ávila, whom he found pensive and sad; he asked him the reason, to which Father John replied: "How blessed you are to live under obedience, and to be sure of doing what God wants. As for me, who can assure me whether it is more pleasing to God for me to go from village to village, instructing the poor peasants, or to stay put in the confessional, hearing the confessions of all the people who come? Those who are living under obedience are sure that, whatever they do when they obey, it is all according to God's will, or rather it is most pleasing to God."[29] Let this serve as a consolation for all those who live under obedience.

18 • Hence for obedience to be perfect, we must obey with our will and our judgment. Obeying with the *will* means obeying voluntarily, and not by constraint, as slaves do; obeying with *judgment* means to align our judgment with the superior's, without scrutinizing what is commanded or how it is commanded. Saint Mary Magdalen de Pazzi said: "Perfect obedience demands a soul without judgment."[30] Likewise Saint Philip Neri said that, in order to obey well, it is not enough to do what obedience commands, but it must be done without question, since we can be sure that what we are bidden is the most perfect thing we can do, even though the opposite were better in the eyes of God.[31]

19 • This holds good not just for religious but also for laypeople under obedience to their spiritual directors. They should have their director assign them all the rules for how to behave both in their spiritual and temporal exercises; that way they will always be sure of doing what is best. As Saint Philip Neri said: "Let those who desire to advance in the way of God submit to a learned confessor, whom they should obey in place of God. By so doing, they can be sure of not having to render an account to God of their actions." He goes on to say, "We must have faith in our confessor, because the Lord would not let him err. There is no surer way to cut through the snares of the devil than to obey the will of others in doing good; and there is nothing more dangerous than to wish to govern ourselves by our own lights."[32]

Likewise, speaking of the guidance provided by the spiritual director as a means of walking safely in the path of perfection, Saint Francis de Sales says, "This is the warning of all warnings: 'Search as much as you like,' says the devout John of Ávila, 'you will never find the will of God so surely as on this path of humble obedience, so much recommended and practiced by all the devout from days of old.'"[33] We are told the same thing by Saint Bernard, Saint Bernardine of Siena, Saint Anthony, Saint John of the Cross, Saint Teresa, Jean de Gerson, and all the theologians and spiritual masters. Saint John of the Cross writes that to doubt this truth is almost as bad as doubting the faith: The words of the saint in his *Treatise on the Thorns* are, "Not to be satisfied with what one's confessor says is pride and a lack of faith."[34] Among the maxims of Saint Francis de Sales we find the following two, which are highly consoling for scrupulous souls: First, no truly obedient person has ever been lost; second, we should be content to be told by our spiritual director that we are making progress, without seeking to have proof of it ourselves.[35]

This is the teaching of many theologians, such as Gerson, Saint Antoninus, Cajetan, Navarro, Sanchez, Bonacina, Corduba, Castropalao, and the Doctors of Salamanca,[36] among others, that the scrupulous person has a serious obligation to resist his or her scruples when there is reason to fear that such scruples will lead to grave damage to soul or body, such as losing one's health or one's mind. For this reason scrupulous persons ought to have more scruples over disobeying their confessor than over fighting their scruples.

To sum up everything that has been said in this chapter, our whole salvation and perfection consist of (1) denying ourselves; (2) following the will of God; (3) and always praying to him for the strength to do both one and the other.

Prayers of Love and Affection

"Whom have I in heaven but you? And there is nothing on earth that I desire other than you;...God is the strength of my heart and my portion for ever" (Ps 73:25–26). My beloved Redeemer, infinitely lovable, since you came down from heaven to give yourself completely to me, what else would I wish for on earth or in heaven besides you, who are the sovereign good, the only good worthy of being loved? Be, then, the only Lord of my heart; possess it entirely: and may my soul love you alone, obey and seek to please you alone. Let others enjoy the riches of this world, I want only you: you are and will be my riches in this life and in eternity. Thus I give you, my Jesus, my whole heart and all my will. It once rebelled against you, but now I consecrate it totally to you. "Lord, what would you have me do?" (Acts 9:6; Vulgate). Tell me what you want of me, and give me your help; for I want to do it all. Dispose of me and what is mine, as it pleases you. I accept everything, and resign myself to everything.

O Love deserving of infinite love, you have loved me to the point of dying for me; I love you with all my heart, I love you more than myself, and into your hands I abandon my soul. Today I renounce all worldly affection; I take my leave of everything created and give myself completely to you. Accept me through the merits of your Passion, and make me faithful to you until death.

My Jesus, my Jesus, from this day forward I want to live only for you. I wish to love none but you, to seek nothing but to do your will. Help me with your grace.

And help me with your protection, O Mary, my hope.

XIV

"Love Bears All Things": Those Who Love Jesus Christ Bear All Things for Jesus Christ, Especially Illness, Poverty, and Contempt

1 • In Chapter V we spoke of the virtue of patience in general. Now we shall deal with certain matters where patience is especially called for.

Father Baltasar Álvarez said that Christians should not think they had made any progress until they had succeeded in holding fast in their heart the sorrows, poverty, and scorn suffered by Jesus Christ, so as to endure with loving patience all pain, sorrow, poverty, and scorn for the sake of Jesus Christ.[1]

In the first place, let us speak of the pains and infirmities of the body, which, when borne with patience, win for us a great crown of merit.

Saint Vincent de Paul said: "If we only knew what a precious treasure is contained in sickness, we would greet it with the same joy as we do the greatest blessings."[2] Hence the saint himself, though he was constantly afflicted by so many ailments that he could often find no rest by night or day, bore them so peacefully and with such a serene expression, without ever complaining, that he seemed to have nothing wrong with him.[3] How edifying it is to see a sick person bearing an illness with a tranquil look on his face, as did Saint Francis de Sales! When he was ill, he simply explained the problem to the doctor, obeyed him without fail by taking all the prescribed medicines, however unpleasant; and then he remained at peace, never complaining about his sufferings.[4] How different this is from some people who never stop complaining at the slightest discomfort, and who would like to have all their relatives and friends cluster around to sympathize with their troubles. By contrast, Saint Teresa exhorted her nuns: "Sisters, learn to suffer something for the love of the Lord, without letting everybody know about it."[5] On one Good Friday, Jesus Christ presented the Venerable Father L. da Ponte with so much physical pain that every part of his body felt its own particular torment. He told a friend about this bitter suffering; but afterward he so regretted it that he vowed never again to reveal his sufferings to anyone.[6]

2 • I say, "Jesus Christ presented him," because the saints consider the sicknesses and pain that God sends them presents. One day Saint Francis of Assisi lay on his bed in excruciating pain. A companion who was assisting him said: "Father, pray God to ease your suffering, and not to lay so heavy a hand upon you." On hearing this, the saint instantly jumped out of bed and knelt down to thank God for his sufferings; then, turning to his companion, he said: "Listen, if I did not know that you said what you did out of simplicity, I would wish never to see you again."[7]

3 • Some sick persons will say: I don't mind suffering this illness so much as the fact that I can't go to church to make my devotions, take Communion, or hear Mass. I can't go to choir to say the Office with my brethren; I can't celebrate

Mass; I can't even pray, because my head is so racked with pain that I feel about to faint. But wait, tell me please: Why do you want to go to church or to choir? Why do you want to receive Communion and say or hear Mass? Is it to please God? But God is pleased now not by your saying the Office or going to Communion or hearing Mass, but by your staying patiently in this bed and suffering the pain of this illness.

But you don't want to hear that; clearly you are not seeking to do what pleases God but what pleases you. John of Ávila wrote to a priest who was complaining in this way: "My friend, don't go adding up all the things you would be doing if you were well, but be content to remain sick as long as it pleases God. If you seek the will of God, what does it matter to you whether you are healthy or sick?"[8]

4 • You say you can't even pray, because you can barely hold your head up. Very well, you can't meditate; but why can't you make acts of resignation to the will of God? If you did, that would be the finest prayer you could ever say, embracing with love all the pain that afflicts you. That was what Saint Vincent de Paul did: when he was gravely ill, he would gently place himself in the presence of God, without forcing his mind to concentrate on any particular subject. All he would do was from time to time make acts now of love, now of trust, now of thanksgiving, and then, still more often, of resignation, whenever the pain increased.[9] Saint Francis de Sales said: "Sufferings in themselves are terrifying; but in the light of God's will, they are lovely and delightful."[10] You can't pray? What finer prayer could there be than to look occasionally at the crucified Jesus Christ, and to offer him the pain you are suffering, joining the little that you endure to the enormous torments that he suffered on the cross?

5 • A holy woman once lay bedridden, afflicted with many troubles. When her maid handed her a crucifix and told her to pray to God to deliver her from the pain, she replied: "How can you ask me to come down from the cross, while I hold in my hands a crucified God? God forbid. I want to suffer for him, who chose to suffer for me pain much worse than mine." This was precisely what Jesus Christ said to Saint Teresa when she was sick and greatly afflicted: he appeared to her all covered with wounds, and then said to her: "Daughter, look at the bitterness of my sufferings, and consider whether yours can be compared with mine."[11] And so the saint used to say when she was in distress from her infirmities: "When I think of all the ways the Lord suffered, though he was completely innocent, I don't know how I could get it into my head to complain of my sufferings."[12]

For thirty-eight years, Saint Lidwine suffered continuously from many diseases, gout in her feet and hands and shingles. But because she always had before her eyes the sufferings of Jesus Christ, she was always lively and cheerful, even though confined to bed.[13] Similarly, when Saint Joseph of Leonessa, a Capuchin, had to undergo an amputation by a surgeon, his brethren wanted to tie him down with ropes to prevent him from moving because of the intense pain. But he took hold of the crucifix and said: "Ropes? Why do I need ropes? Look who is tying me down to suffer in peace all pain for his love," and so he endured the amputation without complaining.[14] Saint Jonas the Martyr, after spending a night encased in ice by order of the tyrant, said the next morning that he had never had a more restful night, because he had pictured to himself Jesus hanging on the cross; and so his sufferings, compared with those of Christ, had seemed more like caresses than torments.[15]

6 • Oh, how much merit can be gained just by patiently enduring sickness! Father Baltasar Álvarez had a vision of the great glory that God had prepared for a devout nun for suffering through a sickness with great patience. He was told that she had earned more merit in the eight months of her illness than some other pious nuns do in many years.[16] It is by patiently enduring the pains of sickness that we win a large, perhaps the largest, part of the crown that God is preparing for us in paradise. That is precisely what was revealed to Saint Lidwine. After suffering through so many painful diseases, as mentioned above, she wished to die a martyr for Jesus Christ. But one day, as she was sighing after this martyrdom, she saw a beautiful crown that was not quite finished; and she understood that it was being readied for herself. In her longing to see it completed, she begged the Lord to increase her sufferings. The Lord answered her prayer by sending some soldiers who brutally mistreated her, not just with insults, but with beatings. Then an angel appeared to her with the crown completed, and told her that those last blows had added to the crown the jewels that were lacking; and shortly afterward she died.[17]

7 • How welcome and sweet are pain and ignominy to souls that ardently love Jesus Christ. That is why the holy martyrs went so gladly to meet the rack, the iron hooks, the burning metal plates, and the meat axes. As he was being tortured by the tyrant, the martyr saint [Procopius] said: "Torment me as much as you like; but know that for those who love Jesus Christ nothing is sweeter than to suffer for his love."[18] Another martyr, Saint Gordianus, told the tyrant who was threatening to have him killed: "You threaten me with death; but my only regret is that I cannot die more than once for my Jesus Christ."[19] Did these saints speak that way because they

were insensible to pain or simply stupid? No, Saint Bernard replies, "It was not stupidity, but love, that did this."[20] They were not insensible; they could very well feel the pain being inflicted on them; but since they loved God, they thought it a great gain to suffer everything and lose everything, including life itself, for the love of God.

8 • In time of sickness especially, we must be ready to accept death, and the death that pleases God. We all must die, and our life must end in our last illness, though we do not know what our last illness will be. So in every illness let us prepare ourselves to embrace the death that God has destined for us.

A sick person may say: "Yes, but I have committed so many sins, and have done no penance. I would like to live, not for the sake of living, but to make some satisfaction to God before I die." But tell me, my friend, how do you know that if you go on living you will do penance, and not do worse than before? Right now you may well hope that God has forgiven you. What finer penance can there be than to accept death with resignation, if God so wills it? Dying young at the age of twenty-three, Saint Aloysius Gonzaga cheerfully embraced death with this reflection: "Just now," he said, "I find myself, I hope, in the grace of God. Afterwards I don't know what may become of me; so I die happy, if now it pleases God to call me to the next life."[21]

Father John of Ávila felt that everyone, even a person of middling virtue, who was properly disposed should desire death, to escape the danger, in which we always live on this earth, of sinning and losing the grace of God.[22]

9 • Besides, owing to our natural weakness, we cannot live in this world without committing at least venial sins. From

this standpoint at any rate, we should cheerfully embrace death, so that we may never offend God anymore. Besides, if we truly love God, we should ardently long to go to see him and love him with all our strength in paradise, which no one can do perfectly in this life. But unless death opens the door for us, we cannot enter that blessed homeland of love. This is why Saint Augustine, who was so in love with God, exclaimed: "Would that I could die, O Lord, that I might see you"[23]: Lord, let me die, because unless I die, I cannot see you and love you face to face.

10 • Second, we must practice patience in enduring poverty. There is certainly a great need for patience when we lack temporal goods. Saint Augustine says: "He who does not have God has nothing; he who has God has everything."[24] Those who have God and are united to the divine will find every good thing. Here is Saint Francis, barefooted, dressed in sackcloth, and poor in every way, who by saying "my God and my all"[25] proved to be happier than all the monarchs of the earth. Those are called poor who desire goods they do not have; but those who desire nothing and are content with their poverty are thoroughly rich. Saint Paul speaks of such people as "having nothing, and yet possessing everything" (2 Cor 6:10). The true lovers of God have nothing and have everything; since, when they lack worldly goods, they say: "My Jesus, you alone are enough for me," and with this they rest content.

Not only did the saints have patience in their poverty, but they sought to be stripped of everything, in order to live detached from everything, and united only to God. If we do not have the courage to renounce all the goods of this world, at least let us be content with the state of life where the Lord wants us to be. And let us not be solicitous for earthly riches, but for heavenly ones, which are immeasurably greater and last forever; and let us persuade ourselves of what Saint Teresa says: "The less we have here, the more we shall enjoy there."[26]

11 • Saint Bonaventure said that an abundance of temporal goods was nothing more than birdlime for the soul, to prevent it from flying to God.[27] And, on the other hand, Saint John Climacus said that poverty is a road on which to travel to God without hindrance.[28]

The Lord said: "Blessed are the poor in spirit, for theirs is the kingdom of heaven" (Mt 5:3). In the other Beatitudes, heaven is promised in the future to the meek and to the pure of heart; but to the poor, heaven, that is, heavenly joy, is promised even in this life: "Theirs is the kingdom of heaven." Yes, for even in this life the poor enjoy a foretaste of paradise. "The poor in spirit" means those who are not just poor in earthly goods, but who do not even desire them. As the apostle Paul says, "But if we have food and clothing, we will be content with these" (1 Tim 6:8).

"Oh, blessed poverty," exclaimed Saint Laurence Giustiniani, "which possesses nothing and fears nothing; it is always joyous and always abundant, since it turns all the troubles it has to the advantage of the soul."[29] Saint Bernard writes: "The covetous person hungers for earthly things like a beggar, the poor person despises them like a lord."[30] The miser is always as ravenous as a beggar, because he never manages to sate himself with the goods he desires; by contrast, the poor man, like a rich lord of all, scorns them, because he desires nothing.

12 • One day Jesus Christ said to Blessed Angela of Foligno: "If poverty were not a great good, I would not have chosen it for myself, nor left it to my chosen ones as their portion."[31]

And, in fact, it is because the saints saw Jesus poor that they have so loved poverty. Saint Paul says, "But those who want to be rich fall into temptation and are trapped by many senseless and harmful desires that plunge people into ruin and destruction" (1 Tim 6:9). Unhappy creatures who, for the wretched goods of this world, forfeit an infinite good, which is God!

So Saint Basil the Martyr was quite right, when the Emperor Licinius proposed to make him his chief priest, if he would abandon Jesus Christ; he was right, I say, to reply: "Tell the emperor that if he were willing to give me his whole kingdom, he couldn't give me as much as he would be taking away from me, by making me lose God."[32] So let us be content with God and with the things he gives us, rejoicing to see ourselves poor when we lack what we would like to have. "It is not poverty that is reckoned a virtue," says Saint Bernard, "but the love of poverty."[33] Many are poor, but because they do not love their poverty, they have no merit. That is why Saint Bernard says that the virtue of poverty consists not in being poor, but in loving poverty.

13 • And religious persons in particular, who have taken a vow of poverty, should have this love of poverty. Many religious, says Saint Bernard, "wish to be poor; so long as they want for nothing."[34] As Saint Francis de Sales says, "They want the honor of poverty, but not its inconveniences."[35] To such people the saying of the Blessed Salomea, a nun of Saint Clare, applies: "A nun who wishes to be poor and then complains when she lacks something will be laughed to scorn by angels and by men."[36] That is not how good nuns behave: they love their poverty above all riches. When the daughter of the Emperor Maximilian II, a discalced nun of Saint Clare known as Sister Margaret of the Cross, appeared before her brother, the Archduke Albert, in a patched-up habit, he voiced his astonishment, as if this were not becoming to her noble birth. But she answered him: "Brother, I am happier with this rag than all the monarchs with their purple robes."[37] Saint Mary Magdalen de Pazzi said: "How fortunate the religious who, detached from everything by means of holy poverty, can say: 'The Lord is my chosen portion' (Ps 16:5). My God, you are my portion and all my good."[38]

Having received many donations from a certain merchant, Saint Teresa sent him word that his name was written in the Book of Life, and that, as a sign of this, the things of this earth would fail him; and in fact the merchant went bankrupt and remained poor until his death.[39] Saint Aloysius Gonzaga said that there could be no surer sign that a person is numbered among the elect than to see him God-fearing and at the same time racked by travail and desolation in this world.[40]

14 • In a way it is yet another feature of holy poverty to be deprived in this life of relatives and friends by death; and here, too, in this we must exercise a great deal of patience. Some people, when they lose a parent or friend, can find no peace. They shut themselves up in their room to weep and, abandoning themselves to their sadness, become so impatient that they become impossible to deal with. I would ask these persons, when they grieve in this way and shed such storms of tears, whom are they trying to please? God? Not God, because God wants us to resign ourselves to his will. The departed soul? Once again, no. If the soul is lost, she hates you and your tears; if she has been saved and is already in heaven, she wishes you to thank God for herself. If she is in purgatory, she desires you to help her with your prayers and to become a saint, so that one day she may have you for a companion in paradise. What good, then, is all that weeping? The Venerable Father Joseph Caracciolo, a Theatine, had lost a brother, and one day he was with other family members who would not stop crying. "Come on," he said, "let us save those tears for a worthier cause, to weep for the death of Jesus Christ, who has been to us a father, a brother, and husband, and who died for love of us."[41]

On such occasions we must act like Job, who, when he heard the news that his children had been killed, completely conformed himself to God's will, and said: "The LORD gave, and the LORD has taken away; blessed be the name of the LORD" (Job 1:21). What has happened was pleasing to God, and so it pleases me too; may he be blessed by me forever.

15 • Third, we must practice patience and show our love for God by peacefully suffering the scorn we receive from others. As soon as souls give themselves completely to God, God himself causes or permits others to despise and persecute them. One day an angel appeared to the Blessed Henry Suso and said to him, "Henry, up till now you have mortified yourself in your own way; from now on you shall be mortified as it will please others." The next day, as he looked out a window, he saw a dog shaking and tearing a rag that it had in its mouth; then he heard a voice saying to him, "That is how you have to be torn by the mouths of men." Blessed Henry went down into the street and got the rag, which he kept for his own comfort in the time of trials that had been foretold to him.[42]

16 • Affronts and injuries are a source of delight that the saints long for and seek out. Saint Philip Neri spent thirty years in Rome at the House of Saint Jerome, where he suffered a great deal of mistreatment from certain individuals. But he refused to leave the house and move to the new Oratory of the

Chiesa Nuova, which he had founded, where his beloved sons had already moved and were inviting him to join them, until he found himself obliged to go there by an express command from the pope.[43] Saint John of the Cross was told he needed a change of air for an illness that later carried him off to the grave. Yet he turned down a more comfortable monastery, where the prior was a close friend of his, and chose instead a poor convent, where the prior was his enemy—a man, in fact, who for a long time, and practically to his dying day, despised him and mistreated him in many ways, even forbidding the other monks to visit him.[44] This is how far the saints go to seek out insults. Saint Teresa wrote this memorable maxim: "Anyone who aspires to perfection must beware of saying: 'They did that to me for no reason.' If you don't want to bear a cross except one supported by reason, then perfection is not for you."[45] When Saint Peter Martyr complained that he had been unjustly imprisoned without having done anything wrong, the crucified Lord gave him a celebrated answer: "And what evil have I done that I had to hang on this cross and suffer and die for men?"[46]

When they have been insulted, the saints derive great consolation from the ignominy that Jesus Christ endured for us. On being asked by his wife how he managed to bear so patiently all the insults he received, even from his own servants, Saint Eleazar replied: "I turn and look on Jesus, who was despised and rejected, and I see that the affronts to me are nothing compared with what he suffered for me; and so God gives me strength to bear it all patiently."[47]

In a word, insults and outrages, poverty, pain and every kind of tribulation befalling a soul that does not love God are only occasions for driving it further from God. But when they befall a soul in love with God, they are motives for clinging more closely to God and loving him more: "Many waters cannot quench love" (Song 8:7). However many and grievous the sufferings may be, not only do they not quench the flames of love, they fan them higher in a heart that loves nothing else but God.

17 • But why does God burden us with so many crosses and take pleasure in seeing us pained, persecuted, and mistreated by the world? Is he, perhaps, a tyrant, whose cruel nature makes him enjoy seeing us suffer? No, God is not a tyrant, nor does he have a cruel nature; he is all pity and love for us. Suffice it to say that he loved us to the point of dying for us. He does rejoice to see us suffer; but that is for our own good, so that by suffering we may be freed from the punishment we would otherwise suffer in the next life for the debts we contracted with divine justice. He rejoices in our suffering so that we may detach ourselves from the sensory pleasures of this world. When a mother wants to wean her baby, she puts gall on her breasts so that the child may find nursing abhorrent. God rejoices in our suffering in hopes that by enduring it with patience and resignation we may give him some proof of our love. Finally, he rejoices in it, so that we may win greater glory in Paradise. These are the reasons, all rooted in pity and love, why the Lord enjoys seeing us suffer.

18 • Let us bring this chapter to an end. If we really wish to practice holy patience in all our tribulations, we must persuade ourselves that all trials come from the hands of God, either directly or indirectly through other human beings. And so when we see ourselves in distress, we must thank the Lord and accept with a cheerful mind whatever he orders for our welfare: "We know that all things work together for good for those who love God" (Rom 8:28).

Furthermore, when we are afflicted by some trial, it helps to look at hell, which we once deserved; for compared with hell, any other suffering will always be infinitely smaller. But to suffer with patience all pain, disgrace, and adversity, prayer is more helpful than any reflection. God's help, which comes after prayer, will give us the strength that we do not have. That is what the saints did. They commended themselves to God, and so overcame all torments and persecutions.

Prayers of Love and Affection

O Lord, I am persuaded that without patient suffering I cannot win the crown of Paradise. David said: "From him is my patience" (Ps 61[62]:6; Vulgate). I say the same: patience in suffering must be your gift to me. I resolve to accept in peace all my tribulations; but no sooner do they arrive than I grow sad and dismayed; and if I suffer, I suffer without merit and without love, because I do not know how to suffer them so as to please you. O my Jesus, through the merits of your patience in suffering so much pain for love of me, grant me the grace to bear crosses for your love.

I love you with all my heart, my dear Redeemer. I love you, my sovereign good. I love you, my love, worthy of infinite love.

Above all other evil, I repent of whatever displeasure I have caused you.

I promise you to accept with patience all the trials that you send me; but from you I hope for your help to carry out my promise, and especially to suffer in peace the pains of my agony and death.

O Mary, my Queen, beg for me true resignation to whatever remains for me to suffer in life and in death.

XV

"Love Believes All Things": Those Who Love Jesus Christ Believe All His Words

1 • A person who loves gives credence to everything the beloved says; and consequently, the greater a soul's love for Jesus Christ, the more solid and lively is the faith of that soul. When the Good Thief saw our Redeemer dying on the cross, though he had done no wrong, and suffering with such patience, he began to love him. Then, inflamed by this love and illumined by the divine light, he believed that this truly was the Son of God, and so begged Jesus to remember him when he came into his kingdom.

2 • Faith is the foundation of love, on which love is built. But love is what brings faith to perfection. The more perfectly we love God, the more perfectly we believe in him. Love makes us believe not just with the intellect but also with the will. Those who believe only with the intellect, but not with the will, are like sinners who know that the truths of faith are only too true, but who do not want to live according to God's commandments. Such people have a very weak faith; because if they had a lively faith and believed that the grace of God is the greatest of good things, and that sin, because it robs us of

God's grace, is the worst of evils, they would surely change their lives. If, therefore, they prefer the miserable goods of this earth to God that is because either they do not believe or they believe very feebly. On the other hand, those who believe with both intellect and will, who not only believe but wish to believe in God, the revealer of truth, out of the love they bear for him, and rejoice in believing—such persons have perfect faith; and hence they try to make their lives conform to the truths that they believe.

3 • But the lack of faith of those who live in sin does not arise from the obscurity of faith. True, God has willed that matters of faith should be dark and hidden to us, so that we may gain merit by believing them. Still the truth of faith has made itself so evident to us by its distinguishing marks, that not to believe them would be not just imprudent, but impious and insane.

Thus the weakness of many people's faith is due to their wicked morals. Those who scorn God's friendship rather than forgo forbidden pleasures would prefer that there were no law to forbid sins and no punishment for sinners. Hence they try to avoid the sight of the eternal truths of death, judgment, hell, and divine justice. Such subjects frighten them too much or embitter their delights, and so they sharpen their wits to find at least some plausible reasons for persuading or flattering themselves that there is no soul, no God, and no hell in order to live and die like the beasts, which have neither law nor reason.

4 • And this laxity of morals is the source that has produced, and continues to produce daily, so many books and systems of materialists, indifferentists, politicists, deists, and naturalists. Some of them deny the existence of God; others

deny divine Providence, saying that God, having once created human beings, takes no further notice of them, and does not care whether they love him or offend him, whether they are saved or lost. Others again deny God's goodness, saying that he has created many souls for hell, that he himself induces them to sin so that they may damn themselves and go off into everlasting fire, to curse him there forever.

5 • See the ingratitude and wickedness of human beings! God has created them in his mercy, to make them eternally happy in heaven; he has heaped on them so many lights, blessings, and graces for them to win eternal life. To the same end he has redeemed them with so much pain and love; and yet they strive to believe nothing, so as to live in vice as they please. But toil as they may, the wretches will never be able to free themselves from the remorse of conscience and the dread of God's vengeance.

On this subject I have recently published a work entitled *The Truth of Faith* (1767), in which I clearly demonstrate the baselessness of all the systems of these modern unbelievers. If only they would give up their vices and apply themselves to loving Jesus Christ, they would certainly stop doubting matters of faith, and firmly believe in all the truths that God has revealed!

6 • Those who love Jesus Christ from the heart always keep the eternal truths before their eyes and direct all their actions accordingly. Those who love Jesus Christ understand well the saying of the Preacher: "Vanity of vanities, all is vanity" (Eccl 1:2). All earthly greatness is smoke, mud, and delusion; the soul's only welfare and happiness consist in loving the Creator and in doing his will. We are no more and no less than what we are before God. It is no use gaining the whole world, if the soul be lost; and all the goods on earth cannot satisfy the human heart, but only God himself. Finally, we must abandon everything to gain everything.

7 • *Love believes all things.* Then there are some other Christians who are not so perverse as those we have mentioned (the ones who would like to believe in nothing so as to live in vice at greater liberty and without remorse), some of these others believe, but their faith is languid. They believe in the most holy mysteries, they believe in the truths revealed in the Gospels, the Trinity, Redemption, the sacraments, and the rest; but they do not believe them all. Jesus Christ has said: "Blessed are you who are poor" (Lk 6:20); "Blessed are those who mourn" (Mt 5:4); "Blessed are those who hunger" (Mt 5:6); "Blessed are those who are persecuted" (Mt 5:10); "Blessed are you when people revile you...and utter all kinds of evil against you" (Mt 5:11). This is how Jesus Christ speaks in the Gospels. But then how can people claim to believe in the Gospels when they say: "Blessed are those who have money. Blessed are those who suffer nothing. Blessed are those who take their pleasure. Ah, the poor person, persecuted and mistreated by others." Such people, it must be said, either do not believe the Gospels or believe them only in part.

Those who believe them entirely consider it a sign of good fortune and God's favor in this world to be poor, to be sick, to be mortified, to be despised and mistreated by others. Such is the belief, and such the language, of those who believe everything that is said in the Gospels and have a real love for Jesus Christ.

Chapter XV

Prayers of Love and Affection

My beloved Redeemer, O life of my soul, I believe that you are the only good worthy of being loved. I believe that you are the greatest lover of my soul, since for love alone you came to die, consumed with pain for love of me. I believe that in this life and the next there is no greater fortune than to love you and to do your will. I firmly believe all this; and so I renounce everything, that I may be wholly yours and have no one but you. Through the merits of your Passion, help me and make of me what you wish.

Infallible truth, I believe in you. Infinite mercy, I trust in you. Infinite goodness, I love you: infinite love, who gave yourself completely to me in your Passion and in the sacrament of the altar, I give myself completely to you.

And I commend myself to you, Mary, refuge of sinners and Mother of God.

XVI

"Love Hopes All Things": Those Who Love Jesus Christ Hope for Everything From Him

1 • Hope increases love, and love increases hope. Hope in God's goodness certainly makes our love grow for Jesus Christ. Saint Thomas writes that as soon as we hope for some benefit from a person, we begin to love him.[1] That is why the Lord doesn't want us to put our trust in creatures: "Do not put your trust in princes" (Ps 146:3). And he curses those who do: "Cursed are those who trust in mere mortals" (Jer 17:5). God doesn't want us to trust creatures, because he doesn't want us to give our love to them. Saint Vincent de Paul said: "Let us be careful not to rely much on the protection of others; because when the Lord sees us leaning on them, he withdraws from us. On the other hand, the more we trust in God, the more we progress in loving him."[2] "I have run the path of your commandments, when you enlarged my heart" (Ps 119:32; Vulgate). Those whose hearts are enlarged by confidence in God run swiftly on the path of perfection. They not only run, they fly; because, having placed all their hope in the Lord, they are no longer weak as they once were. They become strong with the strength of God, which is given to all who put their trust in him: "They who wait for the LORD shall renew their strength, they shall mount up with wings like eagles, they shall run and not be weary, they shall walk and not faint" (Is 40:31). In its soaring flight the eagle comes closest to the sun; and so the soul, strengthened by confidence, takes off from the earth and is joined to God by love.

2 • Now as hope serves to increase love for God, so does love increase hope; for charity makes us the adopted sons and daughters of God. In the natural order we are the work of his hands; but in the supernatural order, thanks to the merits of Jesus Christ, we become children of God, and, as Saint Peter wrote, "participants of the divine nature" (2 Pet 1:4). And if love makes us the sons and daughters of God, it also makes us heirs of heaven, as Saint Paul says: "And if children, then heirs, heirs of God and joint heirs with Christ" (Rom 8:17). Now children are entitled to live in their father's house; heirs are entitled to the inheritance; and thus love increases our hopes of heaven, so that loving souls never stop crying out to God: "Thy kingdom come, thy kingdom come."

3 • Moreover, God loves those who love him: "I love those who love me, and those who seek me diligently find me" (Prov 8:17). He showers his graces on those who lovingly seek him: "The LORD is good to those who wait for him" (Lam 3:25). Consequently, those who love God hope more from his goodness. This intimacy gives the saints the unshakable tranquillity that leaves them joyous and peaceful, even amid adversity; because, loving Jesus Christ as they do, and knowing how generous he is with his gifts to those who love him, they place their trust in him alone, and so they find rest. This is why the spouse in the Song of Solomon was always overflowing with delights, because she loved no one but her beloved, and leaned only on him. Knowing how grateful he is to those who love him, she was perfectly happy; so that Scripture says: "Who is that coming up from the wilderness, leaning upon her beloved?" (Song 8:5). These words of the Sage are most true: "All good things come to me along with her" (Wis 7:11). Along with love, all good things come to the soul.

4 • The primary object of Christian hope is God, whom the souls enjoy in the kingdom of the blessed. But we do not believe that the hope of enjoying God in paradise is any obstacle to love; since the hope of heaven is inseparably connected with love, which is perfected there and finds its full completion. Love is the infinite treasure spoken of by Solomon, "an unfailing treasure for mortals, those who get it obtain friendship with God" (Wis 7:14).

Saint Thomas Aquinas says that friendship is based on the sharing of goods[3]; and, since friendship is nothing but mutual love between friends, they must do good to one another as befits each one. Hence the saint says: "If there were to be no sharing, there would be no friendship"; and Jesus Christ says to his disciples: "I have called you friends, because I have made known to you everything that I have heard from my Father" (Jn 15:15). Since he had made them his friends, he shared all his secrets with them.

5 • Saint Francis de Sales says: "If, by some impossibility there could be an infinite goodness (i.e., a God) to whom we belonged in no way whatever, and with whom we could have no union or communication, we should certainly esteem it greater than ourselves. So we might feel a desire to be able to love it; but we would not love it, because love looks to union. Love is a friendship, and the foundation of friendship is to have things in common; and its goal is union."[4] Thus Saint Thomas teaches that love does not exclude the desire for the reward that God is preparing for us in heaven; on the contrary, it makes us look for it as our chief object, which is God himself, who is enjoyed by the blessed; for friendship implies that friends enjoy one another.[5]

6 • This is the reciprocal sharing that the spouse in the Song of Solomon spoke of: "My beloved is mine and I am his" (Song 2:16). In heaven souls give themselves completely to God, and God gives himself completely to these souls, insofar as they are capable of receiving him, depending upon their merits. But, aware as the souls are of their own nothingness in comparison with the infinite lovableness of God; and hence knowing that God deserves to be loved by them infinitely more than they deserve to be loved by God, they seek God's pleasure more than their own enjoyment. Thus they take more joy in giving themselves completely to God to please him than in God's giving himself completely to them. Meanwhile they are pleased that God gives himself completely to them, insofar as that incites them to give themselves completely to God with a greater intensity of love. They already enjoy the glory that God imparts to them, but only to reflect it back on God himself, and to do their utmost to increase his glory. At the sight of God in heaven, souls cannot help loving him with all their strength; on the other hand, God cannot hate anyone who loves him. But if by some impossibility God could hate a soul that loved him, and if a blessed soul could live without loving God, such souls would much prefer to endure all the pains of hell, provided they were allowed to love God as much as he hated them, rather than to live without loving God, even though they could enjoy all the other delights of Paradise. This is true because souls, knowing that God deserves to be loved infinitely more than they do, have a much greater desire to love God than to be loved by him.

7 • Love hopes all things. As Saint Thomas and Peter Lombard teach us, Christian hope is defined as a "sure expectation of eternal happiness."[6] Its certainty arises from God's infallible promise to give eternal life to his faithful servants. Now love, just as it takes away sin, also removes the obstacles to blessedness. Hence the greater the love, the greater too and the stronger is our hope. On the other hand, hope can certainly never interfere with the purity of love, because, as Dionysius the Areopagite says, love naturally tends to union with the beloved object;[7] or, as Saint Augustine puts it, love itself is like a chain of gold that links the hearts of the lover and the beloved.[8] And as this union can never be achieved at a distance, the one who loves always desires the presence of the beloved. The spouse in the Song of Solomon was languishing far from her beloved and begged her companions to let him know about her pain, so he might come and console her with his presence: "I adjure you, O daughters of Jerusalem, if you find my beloved, tell him this: I am faint with love" (Song 5:8). A soul that loves Jesus Christ exceedingly, while living on this earth, can only desire and hope to go quickly to heaven and be united with the beloved Lord.

8 • Thus the desire to go and see God in heaven, not so much for the pleasure that we shall experience in loving God, as for the pleasure that we shall give God by loving him, is pure and perfect love. Nor is the joy of the blessed in heaven at loving God any hindrance to the purity of their love. Such joy is inseparable from love; but the blessed find far greater pleasure in their love of God than in the joy they feel in loving him. Someone might say: Is not the desire for a reward a selfish love rather than a love of friendship? But one must distinguish here between temporal rewards promised by human beings and the reward of Paradise promised by God to those who love him. The rewards given by humans are distinct from their own persons, since humans, when they reward others, do not give themselves, but only their goods. By contrast, the principal reward that God gives to the blessed is the gift of himself: "I am your shield; your reward shall be very great" (Gen 15:1). So desiring heaven is the same as desiring God, who is our ultimate goal.

9 • Here I wish to mention a doubt that may readily occur to those souls who love God and are trying to conform themselves in all things to God's blessed will. Should it be ever revealed to such persons that they would be eternally damned, would they be obliged to accept this, so as to be in conformity with the will of God? Saint Thomas says no; in fact, he teaches that anyone who consented would be sinning, because that person would be consenting to live in a state that necessarily involves sin, and is contrary to the ultimate goal for which God created us. God did not create souls to hate him in hell, but to love him in Paradise: and so he wishes no one's death, not even the sinner's, but that all should convert and be saved. Saint Thomas says that God wishes no one to be damned except for sin; and so if a person consented to his own damnation, he would not be acting in conformity with the will of God, but with the will of sin.[9]

But what if God, foreseeing someone's sin, had decreed his damnation, and what if this decree should be revealed to the person: would he be bound to consent to it? In the same passage the saint says, not even then; because such a revelation should not be understood as an irrevocable decree, but merely as a threat of what will happen if a person persists in sin.

10 • But let everyone banish from his or her mind such gloomy thoughts, which serve only to put a chill on confidence and love. Let us love Jesus Christ as much as we can here below; let us forever sigh to go see him in Paradise, so that there we may love him perfectly. Let this be the chief object of all our hopes, to go there to love him with all our might. Even in this life we have the commandment: "You shall love the Lord your God with all your heart, and with all your soul, and with all your strength, and with all your mind" (Lk 10:27). But Thomas Aquinas says that this precept cannot be perfectly fulfilled by human beings on this earth.[10] Only Jesus Christ, who was both God and man, and his holy Mother Mary, who was full of grace and free from original sin, carried it out perfectly. But we wretched children of Adam, infected as we are with sin, cannot love God without some imperfection; and only in heaven, when we shall see God face to face, shall we love him—indeed we shall have to love him—with all our strength.

11 • Here, then, is the goal that all our longings, sighs, thoughts, and hopes must aim for: to go and enjoy God in Paradise in order to love him with all our might and to rejoice in the enjoyment of God. The blessed certainly enjoy their own happiness in that kingdom of delights; but their chief enjoyment, which absorbs all the other delights, is to know the infinite happiness that their beloved Lord enjoys, while they love God immeasurably more than themselves. All the blessed have such love for him that they would happily forfeit all delights and suffer any pain, rather than see God miss (if that were possible) one tiny particle of the happiness he enjoys. Thus paradise for them is seeing God's infinite happiness and knowing that it can never fail for all eternity. This is the meaning of what the Lord says to every soul whom he welcomes into glory: "Enter into the joy of your master" (Mt 25:21). The joy does not enter into the blessed, but the blessed enter into the joy of God, since the joy of God is the object of the joy of the blessed. Thus what is precious to God will be precious to the blessed; the riches of God will be their riches, and the happiness of God will be their happiness.

12 • The moment that souls enter heaven and see in the light of glory the infinite beauty of God, they find themselves wholly possessed and consumed with love. Then the blessed remain happily lost and immersed in the infinite ocean of God's goodness. They forget themselves, and, inebriated with divine love, think only of loving their God: "They feast on the abundance of your house, and you give them drink from the river of thy delights" (Ps 37:8). Just as drunkards no longer think of themselves, so the souls in bliss can think only of loving and pleasing their beloved; they long to possess him completely, and they do possess him completely, never fearing to lose him again. They desire to give all of themselves to him, at every moment; and they get their wish, because at every moment they give all of themselves to God without reserve; and God embraces them with love; he holds them, and will hold them, in that embrace for all eternity.

13 • Thus in heaven souls are wholly united to God, and love him with all their strength, with a love that is consummate and complete. And although this love is finite, since creatures are not capable of infinite love, it nevertheless makes them perfectly happy and contented, so that they desire nothing more. On the other hand, God communicates with these souls and joins himself completely to them, filling them with himself as much as their merits allow. And he unites himself to them not just by means of his gifts, lights, and loving appeals, as he does with us in this life, but with his very essence. As fire penetrates a bar of iron, and seems to transform it into itself, so God penetrates these souls and fills them with himself. And though they never lose their own essential being, they still become so saturated and absorbed into that immense ocean of the divine substance that they are left, as it were, drowned and annihilated. This was the happy fate that the apostle Paul prayed his disciples might have: "That you may be filled with all the fullness of God" (Eph 3:19).

14 • And this is the final goal that the Lord, in his goodness, has appointed for us in the next life. Hence the soul can never fully rest here on earth, until it joins God in heaven, where there is perfect union. It is true that in conforming themselves to God's will, the lovers of Jesus Christ find their peace. But in this life they cannot find complete rest, because they attain that only when they attain their last end, which is seeing God face to face and being consumed by his love. And until souls reach this end, they are restless; they groan and sigh: "Surely, it was for my welfare that I had great bitterness" (Is 38:17).

15 • Yes, my God, I do live in peace in this vale of tears, because that is your will; but I cannot help feeling inexpressible bitterness at seeing myself so far from you, and still not perfectly united to you, who are my center, my everything, my full and final rest.

That is why the saints, though they all burned with love for God on this earth, constantly sighed for Paradise. David cried out: "Woe is me, that my sojourning is prolonged!" (Ps 120:5; Vulgate). "When I awake, I shall be satisfied, beholding your likeness" (Ps 17:15). Saint Paul said of himself: "My desire is to depart and be with Christ" (Phil 1:23). Saint Francis of Assisi said, "So very great / is the good I await, / that every pain / strikes me as gain."[11]

These were all so many acts of perfect charity. Saint Thomas Aquinas teaches that the highest degree of love to which a soul can ascend in this life is an intense desire to go and be united with God, and to enjoy him in heaven.[12] But, as we have said, this enjoyment of God in heaven is not so much a question of the souls' receiving the pleasure that God gives them there as of the pleasure they take in the pleasure of God himself, whom they love incomparably more than themselves.

16 • The greatest pain felt by the holy souls in purgatory is their yearning for God, whom they do not possess. And this pain will bring special distress to souls who in their lifetime yearned but little for Paradise. Cardinal Bellarmine says that in purgatory there is a place called *the prison of honor,* where certain souls suffer not from any pain of the senses, but only from the deprivation of the sight of God.[13] A number of examples of this are recounted by Saint Gregory the Great, the Venerable Bede, Saint Vincent Ferrer, and Saint Bridget. And this punishment is not for any sins committed, but for a lack of desire for heaven. Many souls aspire to perfection, but they are too indifferent about whether they wish to go to see God or continue to live on this earth. But eternal life is the supreme benefit that Jesus Christ has won for us with his death, which is why he punishes souls who during their lives have had too little desire for it.

Prayers of Love and Affection

God, my Creator and my Redeemer, you created me for heaven; you redeemed me from hell to bring me to Paradise; yet by offending you so often I have renounced heaven to your face, and I have been content to see myself condemned to hell. But blessed forever be your infinite mercy that by pardoning me—as I hope—has so many times torn me from hell. Ah, my Jesus, would that I had never offended you! Would that I had always loved you! I am glad that I still have time to do so.

I love you, love of my soul. I love you with all my heart; I love you more than my life itself.

I see that you wish to save me, so that I may love you for all eternity in the kingdom of love. I thank you and beg you to help me for the rest of my life, during which I wish to love you greatly, in order to love you greatly in eternity.

My Jesus, when will the day come when I shall find myself free from the danger of ever losing you again, and consumed by love for you as I see revealed your infinite beauty, so that I shall have to love you? Oh, sweet necessity! Oh, happy, beloved, and longed-for necessity, which will relieve me from all fear of displeasing you, and will compel me to love you with all my might!

My conscience frightens me, and asks me: "How can you expect to enter heaven?" But, my dearest Redeemer, your merits are my hope.

O Mary, Queen of Heaven, your intercession is all powerful with God. In you I trust.

XVII

"Love Endures All Things": Those Who Love Jesus Christ With a Strong Love Do Not Stop Loving Him Amid All Temptations and Desolation

1 • The pain that in this life chiefly afflicts the souls that love God does not come from poverty, sickness, dishonor, and persecution, but from temptations and desolation of spirit. When souls enjoy the loving presence of God, then all the sufferings, ignominy, and mistreatment by others, rather than afflicting them, console them, giving them grounds for offering God a pledge of their love. The pledges are, in short, fuel to make the fire burn brighter. But to find themselves thrust by temptations into losing God's grace, or fearing in desolation that they have already lost it, these pains are too bitter for those who love Jesus Christ. But the same love supplies them with strength to endure afflictions patiently and to continue on the path of perfection that they have already chosen. And indeed how far souls advance with the trials that God sends them to test their love!

Temptations

2 • For the souls that love Jesus Christ there is no greater torment than temptations. If they are accepted with resignation, all the other evils press souls on to closer union with God. But temptations drive us to sin, as mentioned above, and to separation from Jesus Christ. And for this reason they are more bitter than all the other afflictions.

We must understand, however, that none of the temptations that lead us into evil ever come from God, but only from the devil or our own evil inclinations: "God cannot be tempted by evil and he himself tempts no one" (Jas 1:13). Nevertheless the Lord sometimes permits his most beloved souls to be most severely tempted.

He does so, in the first place, in order that from temptations souls may better learn their weaknesses and their need for divine help if they are not to fall. When souls find themselves favored by God with divine consolations, they feel as if they could beat back every assault by their enemies and carry out every enterprise for the glory of God. But when they are strongly tempted, and see themselves at the edge of the cliff and about to fall, then they better understand how wretched they are and how powerless to resist, unless God comes to the rescue. This is precisely what happened to Saint Paul, who wrote: "And to keep me from being too elated, a thorn was given me in the flesh, a messenger of Satan, to torment me" (2 Cor 12:7).

3 • Furthermore, God permits temptations so that we may live more detached from this earth and desire more ardently to go see him in Paradise. Hence when they see themselves attacked in this life day and night by so many enemies, good souls find life tedious and cry out: "Woe is me that my sojourning is prolonged" (Ps 119:5; Vulgate). And they sigh for the hour when they can say: "The snare is broken and we have escaped" (Ps 124:7). These souls would wish to fly to God; but as long as they live upon earth they are bound by a snare that holds them down here, where they are constantly assailed by temptations. This snare can be broken only by death: and so loving souls sigh for death to free them from the danger of losing God.

4 • Moreover God allows us to be tempted, to make us richer in merits, as Tobias was told: "And because you were acceptable to God, it was necessary that temptation should prove you" (Tob 12:13; Vulgate). Thus souls must not fear that they have fallen out of favor with God because they are tempted. Instead they must hope all the more to be loved by God. It is a trick of the devil to make some fainthearted spirits believe that temptations are sins that dirty the soul. It is not evil thoughts that make us lose God, but evil consent to them. Let the suggestions of the devil be ever so overwhelming, let the impure fantasies that flood the mind be ever so lively, when we reject them, they do not leave the slightest stain on our souls. On the contrary they make the soul purer, stronger, and dearer to God.

Saint Bernard says that every time we overcome a temptation, we win a new crown.[1] An angel once appeared to a Cistercian monk, and put a crown into his hands, with orders that he should take it to one of his fellow religious and tell him that he had gained the crown because of the temptation that he had lately overcome.[2] Nor should we be frightened if the evil thought does not leave our mind and continues to torment us. It is enough that we abhor it and try to drive it off.

5 • "God is faithful," says the apostle Paul, "and he will not let you be tested beyond your strength, but with the testing he will also provide the way out so that you may be able to endure it" (1 Cor 10:13). Thus a person who resists temptation not only loses nothing by it, but profits greatly ("with the temptation [he] will also provide the way of escape"). That is why God often allows the souls dearest to him to be the most tried by temptations, that they may acquire more merit on this earth and more glory in heaven. Stagnant water soon goes bad; and souls that stand idle, without any temptations and combats, are in danger of perishing from vain complacency about their own merit; perhaps they think they have already reached perfection, and so have little fear, seldom commend themselves to God, and make little effort to secure their salvation. But when they are shaken by temptations and see themselves in danger of plunging into sin, then they have recourse to God and to the divine Mother; they renew their resolution to die rather than to sin; they humble themselves and abandon themselves to the embrace of God's mercy. In this way, as experience shows, the soul grows stronger and comes closer to God.

6 • This, however, is no reason for us to desire temptations. Instead we must always pray to God to deliver us from temptation, and especially from those that God sees would overcome us. That is why we pray in the Our Father, "Lead us not into temptation." But when God permits them to attack us, we must then, without getting either alarmed or discouraged by those foul thoughts, place our trust in Jesus Christ and seek his help. And he will surely not fail to give us the strength to resist. Saint Augustine says: "Abandon yourself to God and fear not, because if he puts you in the battle, he certainly will not leave you there just so you can fall."[3]

7 • We come now to the means that must be used to vanquish temptations.

Spiritual masters point to a wide variety of means; but the safest and the most necessary—and the only one that I want to mention here—is to turn to God with all humility and confidence, saying: "Be pleased, O God, to deliver me! O LORD, make haste to help me!" (Ps 70:1). This prayer all by itself will be enough to let us overcome the assaults of all the demons in hell; because God is infinitely stronger than they are. God already knows that we ourselves lack the power to resist the temptations of the infernal powers. Hence the learned Cardinal Vincent Gotti says that whenever we are locked in combat and in danger of being overcome, God is obliged to give us enough help to resist so long as we ask him for it.[4]

8 • And how can we fear that Jesus Christ might not help us, after all the promises he has made to us in holy Scripture? "Come to me, all you that are weary and are carrying heavy burdens, and I will give you rest" (Mt 11:28). Come to me, you who are worn out from fighting temptations, and I will restore your strength. "Call on me in the day of trouble: I will deliver you, and you shall glorify me" (Ps 50:15). When you find yourself troubled by your enemies, call upon me, and I will get you out of the danger, and you will praise me for it. "Then you shall call, and the LORD will answer; you shall cry

for help, and he will say, Here I am" (Is 58:9). "Has anyone trusted in the Lord and been disappointed?" (Sir 2:10). David felt sure that, if he turned to prayer, he would never be conquered by his enemies; he says: "I call upon the LORD...so I shall be saved from my enemies" (Ps 18:3). For he knew that "The LORD is near to all who call on him" (Ps 145:18). And Saint Paul adds, that the Lord "is generous to all who call on him" (Rom 10:12).

9 • Would to God that all men and women turn to him whenever they are tempted to offend him; if they did, surely no one would ever offend him. The wretches fall because, lured by their vicious appetites, they would rather lose God, the sovereign good, than their short-lived pleasures. Experience clearly shows that those who look to God in time of temptation do not fall; and that those who turn away, do fall. This is especially true of temptations to impurity. Solomon said, "And, as I knew that I could not contain my passions, unless God gave me the gift...I went to the Lord and begged him" (Wis 8:21; Vulgate). In such cases—and the same holds for temptations against faith—the rule is never to fight the temptation head to head. We must strive from the beginning to dislodge it indirectly by making an act of love for God or of sorrow for our sins, or else by applying ourselves to some indifferent business by way of distraction. As soon as we become aware of a thought that has an evil look about it, we must dismiss it immediately. We must, as it were, slam the door in its face, denying it admittance into the mind, without stopping to decipher its meaning or intention. We must shake off such wicked suggestions as quickly as we would shake off fiery sparks that landed on our clothes.

10 • If the impure thought has already forced its way into the mind and made it clear what it wants, so as to stir the senses, then, says Saint Jerome, "We must cry aloud: O Lord, my helper."[5] The moment, he says, that our senses are moved by the provocation, we must turn to God and say: "O Lord, help me," invoking the most holy names of Jesus and Mary, which have a special power to suppress this kind of temptation.

Saint Francis de Sales says that when children see a wolf they instantly run to the arms of their father and mother, and stay there safe and sound. That is what we must do: immediately turn to Jesus and Mary, calling upon them by name.[6] I repeat, turn to them immediately, without listening to the temptation or arguing with it. In the book *Sentences of the Fathers,* we are told that one day Saint Pacomius heard the devil boasting that he had often gotten the better of a certain monk, because when he tempted him, the monk listened to him and never had recourse to God. By contrast, he heard another devil complaining, "I get nowhere with my monk, because he immediately turns to God and always defeats me."[7]

11 • Should the temptation persist in bothering us, let us beware of becoming troubled or angry at it; for the devil might draw the strength from this sort of disturbance to make us fall. We must humbly resign ourselves to the will of God, who wishes to let us be so tormented by that obscene thought; and we must say: "O Lord, I deserve to be troubled by these disgusting things, as a punishment for my offenses against you. But you must help and set me free." And so, if the temptation continues to bother us, let us continue to call on Jesus and Mary. It is also very useful, if the temptation still torments us, to renew our promise to God to suffer every affliction and to die a thousand deaths rather than offend him; and at the same time there must be no letup in seeking his help.

Should the temptation be so strong as to put us in great danger of consenting to it, we must then redouble our prayers, go to the Blessed Sacrament, throw ourselves at the feet of the crucifix or of some image of the Blessed Virgin, and pray with greater fervor, and groan and weep as we plead for help. God is certainly ready to hear those who pray to him; and it is this, not our own efforts, that must give us the strength to resist. But sometimes the Lord wants these exertions from us; and then he makes up for our weakness by granting us the victory.

12 • It also helps in time of temptation to make the sign of the cross several times on the forehead and breast. And it greatly helps to tell one's spiritual director about the temptation. Saint Philip Neri used to say that a temptation disclosed is half defeated.[8]

But here it is worth noting that theologians, even of the rigorist school, generally admit that persons who have long led a spiritual life and greatly fear God, so long as they are in doubt whether they have consented to a grievous sin, should feel sure that they have not lost God's grace. It is morally impossible that a will whose good intentions have been tried and tested for a long time should all of a sudden change and consent to a mortal sin without clearly realizing it. Mortal sin is so hideous a monster that it could not enter a soul that has long abhorred it, without the soul's full awareness. We have proved this at length in our *Moral Theology*.[9] Saint Teresa said: "No one is lost without knowing it; and no one is deceived without wanting to be deceived.[10]

13 • Therefore, in the case of souls with a delicate conscience and a solid grounding in virtue, but timid and bothered by temptations (especially against faith or chastity), the director will sometimes find it appropriate to forbid them to reveal or make any mention of their temptations. This is because, if they have to mention them they will be forced to reflect on how such thoughts made their way into their minds, and then whether they took any delectation in discussing them, whether they had any pleasure or gave any consent to them. And thus the more they think about these evil fantasies, the more the latter will be imprinted in their minds, and the more they will be disturbed.

When the confessor is morally certain that the penitent has not consented to such temptations, the best way is to forbid him or her to speak about them. I find that Saint Jane Frances de Chantal took precisely this approach. She reports that she herself was for some years tossed about by the most violent storms of temptation, but since she was not aware of ever having ever given in to them, she never spoke of them in confession, in keeping with advice of her spiritual director. She says, "I never had a clear awareness of having consented."[11] Her language suggests that the temptations caused her some disturbance, on account of scruples; but despite that she found calm, thanks to her director's insistence that she not confess such doubts. Otherwise, generally speaking, to suppress temptations, it is very helpful to reveal them to one's confessor, as mentioned above.

14 • But I repeat, the most effective and most necessary of all remedies against temptations, the remedy of remedies, is to pray to God for help, and to continue praying as long as the temptation lasts. Often the Lord will have decreed that victory will come, not at the first prayer, but at the second, third, or fourth. In short, we must persuade ourselves that all our welfare depends on prayer; changing our lives depends on prayer; conquering temptations depends on prayer; obtaining divine love—along with perfection, perseverance, and eternal salvation—depends upon prayer.

15 • Some readers familiar with my spiritual works may find it tedious to hear me so often recommending the importance and necessity of constantly turning to God in prayer. But, for my part, I seem to have said not too much, but far too little. I know that day and night we are all assailed by temptations from hell, and that the devil never misses a chance to make us fall. I know that without God's help we do not have the strength to resist the attacks of the devils, and that hence the apostle Paul exhorts us: "Put on the whole armor of God, so that you may be able to stand against the wiles of the devil. For our struggle is not against enemies of blood and flesh, but against the rulers, against the authorities, against the cosmic powers of this present darkness, against the spiritual forces of evil in heavenly places" (Eph 6:11–12).

And what is this armor Saint Paul teaches us to put on to resist the demons? "Pray in the Spirit at all times in every prayer and supplication. To that end keep alert and always persevere in supplication" (Eph 6:18). The armor is constant and fervent prayer to God, that he may help us and that we may not be conquered. I know, moreover, that all Scriptures, both in the Old and the New Testaments, never stop admonishing us to pray: "Call upon me in the day of trouble; I will deliver you" (Ps 50:15). "Call to me and I will answer you" (Jer 33:3). "Then Jesus told them a parable about their need to pray always and not to lose heart" (Lk 18:1). "Ask, and it will be given you" (Mt

7:7). "Stay awake and pray" (Mt 26:41). "Pray without ceasing" (1 Thes 5:17). So again it seems to me that I have not said too much about prayer, but far too little.

16 • I would wish for all preachers to commend nothing so much to their hearers as prayer; and the same for confessors: there is nothing they should urge upon their penitents so fervently as prayer; and for spiritual writers: there is no topic they should discuss more often than prayer. But I deeply regret the fact—and this seems to me a punishment for our sins—that so many preachers, confessors, and writers have so little to say about prayer. There is no doubt that sermons, meditations, holy Communion, and mortification are a great help to the spiritual life. But if, when temptations come, we don't commend ourselves to God, we shall fall, in spite of all the sermons, all the meditations, all the Communions, all the penances, and all the good resolutions. Therefore if we wish to be saved, let us always pray and commend ourselves to our Redeemer Jesus Christ, especially when we are tempted. And let us not only ask him for final perseverance, but at the same time for the grace to pray to him always. And let us always commend ourselves to the divine Mother, who is the dispenser of grace, as Saint Bernard says, "Let us seek grace, and let us seek it through Mary."[12] The same saint tells us that it is God's will that all the graces we receive pass through the hands of Mary.[13]

Prayers of Love and Affection

Jesus, my Redeemer, I hope by your blood that you have forgiven me my offenses against you; and I hope to come one day to thank you for it forever in Paradise. "I will sing of your steadfast love, O LORD, forever" (Ps 89:1). I see that in the past I have miserably fallen and fallen again, because I have been negligent in asking you for holy perseverance. I now seek this perseverance: "Never let me be separated from you." And I resolve to ask it of you always, but especially when I am tempted to offend you. This is what I resolve and promise, but what good will my resolutions and promises do me, unless you give me the grace to rush back to your feet? By the merits of your Passion, grant me this grace, always to commend myself to you in all my needs.

O Mary, my queen and mother, I pray you, by all your love for Jesus Christ, to obtain this grace for me: always to turn to your Son and to you as long as I live.

Desolation

17 • "It is an illusion," says Saint Francis de Sales, "to try to measure devotion by the consolations that we experience. True devotion on the way to God consists in having a resolute will to do all that is pleasing to God."[14] God uses times of aridity to press his most beloved souls closer to him. What hinders true union with God is attachment to our disordered inclinations. When, therefore, God wants to draw souls to his perfect love, he tries to detach them from all affection for created goods. And so first of all he takes away from them temporal goods, worldly pleasures, possessions, honors, friends, relatives, and bodily health. By the loss of such things, through disgust, disparagement, troubles, deaths and illnesses, and infirmities, he gradually detaches souls from all that is created, to get them to place all their affections in him.

18 • Then to make them fond of spiritual things, God at first lets them taste many consolations, with an abundance of tears and tenderness. As a result souls seek to move away from sensual pleasures; instead they try to mortify themselves with penances, fasts, hair shirts, and disciplines. But here the director should keep these souls in check and not let them do mortifications, at least not all the ones they ask for, because people driven by intense fervor could easily ruin their health through indiscretion. This is a stratagem of the devil. When he sees that someone is giving himself to God and realizes that God is consoling the person with caresses usually given to beginners, the enemy seeks to make him lose his health through excessive penance. That way, when sickness comes, he will give up not just penances, but prayer, Communion, all devout exercise, and return to his old way of life.

For this reason the director, when dealing with souls who have just begun a spiritual life and are looking for penances to do, should be very sparing in permitting them. The spiritual director should seek rather to exhort them to mortify themselves interiorly, by patiently suffering affronts and adversity, by obeying superiors, by restraining the curiosity to see, to hear, and things like that. And the director should tell them that when they have gotten into the habit of practicing these inner mortifications, they will then be able to make themselves worthy of outer ones.

Moreover it is a terrible mistake to say, as some do, that external mortifications are of little or no use. No doubt, inner mortification is more necessary for perfection, but that does not mean that outer mortifications are not needed too.

Saint Vincent de Paul declared that those who do not practice external mortifications will be mortified neither within or without.[15] And Saint John of the Cross added that a director who despises mortification of the flesh should not be trusted, even if he could work miracles.[16]

19 • But to get back to the point. When souls first give themselves to God and taste the sweetness of the sensible consolations with which the Lord seeks to allure them and thus win them away from earthly pleasures, they begin breaking off their attachment to creatures, and become attached to God. Still, this attachment is imperfect, since they are prompted more by feelings of spiritual consolation than by the genuine will to do what is pleasing to God. And they deceive themselves by believing that the more pleasure they take in their devotions, the more they love God. Consequently, when they are kept from those exercises where they used to find a pleasant pasture, and are employed in other works of obedience or charity or the duties of their state, they are disturbed and deeply distressed.

This is a universal defect in our wretched human nature, that in everything we do we seek our own gratification. Or else, when we no longer find in our devout exercises the pleasures we tasted before, we either abandon them or at least cut back on them, and after reducing them from day to day, at last we drop them completely. And this misfortune befalls many souls who, when called by God to love him, enter upon the path of perfection and, as long as spiritual sweetness lasts, make some progress. But when these sensations fade, they abandon everything, and go back to their former ways. We must, however, be persuaded that the love of God and perfection do not consist in feeling tenderness and consolation, but in overcoming self-love, and in following the will of God. Saint

Francis de Sales says: "God is just as lovable when he afflicts us as when he consoles us.[17]

20 • When one is in a state of consolation, it takes no great virtue to forgo sensual pleasures and to endure affronts and adversity. A soul that is awash in this sweetness can endure anything; but such endurance often derives more from those sweet consolations than from the strength of true love for God. And so the Lord, in order to give the soul a solid foundation in virtue, withdraws and takes away sensory pleasures, that he may rid the soul of all attachment to self-love, which feeds on such pleasures. And hence it happens that, although before this the soul felt joy in making acts of self-sacrifice, of confidence, and of love, afterward, once the vein of consolation has dried up, the soul makes these acts with coldness and difficulty and feels boredom in the most devout exercises, in prayer, spiritual reading, and Communion. On the contrary, the soul finds nothing in them but darkness and fears, and all seems lost. The soul prays and prays again, and is grieved, because God seems to refuse to hear.

21 • We come now to what we must do for our part.

When the Lord in his mercy consoles us with loving visitations and makes us feel the presence of his grace, it is not good to reject these divine consolations, as some false mystics would have us do. Let us receive them with gratitude, but let us beware of dwelling on them, to taste and enjoy the feeling of these tender spiritual delights. Saint John of the Cross calls this attitude "spiritual gluttony"; it is a fault and displeasing to God.[18] So let us take care in such moments to expel from our mind any indulgence in this sweetness, and let us especially beware of supposing that God gives us these favors because we are on better terms with him than others. Such vain thinking would force God to withdraw himself from us altogether and leave us in our wretchedness. At such times we must, indeed, thank him fervently, because such spiritual consolations are great gifts from God to souls, far greater than all temporal riches and honors. But when they come, let us not seek delight in those pleasures of sense. Let us humble ourselves by recalling to mind the sins of our past life. We must consider this loving treatment purely and simply the result of God's goodness. Perhaps the Lord is comforting us with these joys by way of anticipation, so that later we may patiently suffer some great tribulation that he wishes to send us. And so let us offer ourselves up to suffer every pain, internal or external, that may come our way, every sickness, every persecution, every spiritual desolation, saying: "My Lord, here I am. Do with me, and with what is mine, whatever you wish. Give me the grace to love you and to carry out your will perfectly, and I ask no more."

22 • When souls are morally certain of being in the grace of God, although they may be deprived of both worldly and godly pleasures, still they are content with their state, knowing, as they do, that they love God and are loved by him. But God wishes to see them more purified and stripped of all sensory enjoyment in order to unite them entirely to himself by means of pure love. What does God do? He puts them in the crucible of desolation, which is a pain more bitter than the worst agony, internal or external, that a person can suffer. He deprives them of the knowledge that they are in the state of grace, and leaves them in darkness so thick that it seems the soul will never find God. Still worse, God will sometimes allow souls to be assaulted by violent sensual temptations, accompanied by evil impulses from their lower depths, or by thoughts of unbelief, despair, and even hatred of God. It will seem to them that the Lord has driven them off and that he no longer hears their prayers. On the one hand, the suggestions of the devil have overwhelming power, and the person's concupiscence is excited, and, on the other, the soul finds itself in deep darkness. As a result, even though the soul's will resists, it cannot clearly discern whether it is resisting the temptations as it should or is giving in to them. This greatly increases the souls' fear that they have lost God or that God has completely, and rightly, abandoned them, because of their betraying him in those struggles. Hence they seem to have already plunged into the depths of ruin, to love God no longer, and to be hated by him. Saint Teresa tasted this pain to the fill; and the saint confesses that when she was in this state, solitude no longer consoled, but tormented her, while praying seemed to her a perfect hell.[19]

23 • When this happens to souls that love God, they should not be dismayed, nor should their director become alarmed. Those sensual stirrings, those temptations against faith, those feelings of distrust, and those attacks that urge them to hate God, are fears, are torments of the soul, are efforts by the enemy; but they are not voluntary acts, and hence they are not sins. The soul that truly loves Jesus Christ does resist and refuse such suggestions; but because of the encompassing darkness the soul cannot see clearly. The soul remains confused and, because it feels abandoned by the presence of grace, the soul is fearful and dejected. But it soon becomes apparent that in these souls, put to the test by God, all is fright and misgivings, but not truth: just ask them, even in their state of abandonment, whether they would knowingly commit one single deliberate venial sin. They will firmly reply that they are ready to suffer not one but a thousand deaths, rather than deliberately cause such displeasure to God.

24 • So we have to make a distinction: it is one thing to perform a good act, such as fending off temptation, trusting in God, loving God, and willing what God wills; and it is another thing to know that we are in fact performing that good act. The second serves for our enjoyment, but the profit lies in the first, that is, in actually doing good. God is satisfied with the first, and deprives the soul of the second, the consciousness of having done good, in order to take away all self-satisfaction, which really adds nothing to the merit of the action. The Lord seeks our advantage more than our satisfaction. Saint John of the Cross wrote to console a soul in desolation: "You have never been in better condition than now; for you have never been so humiliated and detached from the world; and never before have you realized how bad you are. Nor have you ever been so dispossessed and far removed from self-seeking."[20] So we should not believe that when we feel more spiritual tenderness, we are more beloved by God; for perfection does not consist in that, but in mortifying our will and in uniting it to the will of God.

25 • Thus in the state of desolation souls must not heed the devil when he suggests that God has abandoned them; and they must never stop praying. That is what the devil is aiming at, so as to thrust them down some precipice. Saint Teresa wrote: "The Lord tests his lovers by dryness and temptations. Even though the dryness should last a lifetime, the soul should never abandon prayer. The time will come when everything will be fully repaid."[21] In such a state of suffering, a person must humble himself with the thought that he deserves to be treated this way for his offenses against God. He should humble himself, and be fully resigned to God's will, saying: "Here I am, O Lord; if you want me to be desolate and afflicted this way all my life, and even for all eternity, give me your grace, make me love you, and then do with me what you will."

26 • It will be useless, then, and perhaps only cause greater anxiety, to try to assure yourself that you are in God's grace, and that what you are going through is only a trial and not abandonment by God, because God does not want you to know that. And he wants to keep you ignorant for your own advantage, so that you may further humble yourself and increase your prayers and acts of confidence in his mercy. You want to see, but God does not want you to see. Moreover Saint Francis de Sales says: "The resolution not to consent to any sin, however small, assures us that we are in God's grace."[22]

Yet when souls are in deep desolation they cannot even know *that* clearly. But in such a state they must not insist upon feeling what they want. It is enough to wish for it with the tip of their wills. Thus they must entirely abandon themselves into the arms of God's goodness. God is enchanted by such acts of trust and resignation amid the darkness of desolation. Indeed, let us put our trust in a God, who, as Saint Teresa says, loves us far more than we love ourselves.[23]

27 • Therefore these souls so dear to God and resolved to be entirely his, even as they see themselves bereft of every consolation, should take comfort. Their desolation is a sign of their being greatly loved by God, and that he has prepared a place for them in Paradise, where the consolations are total and everlasting. And let them take it for a certainty that the more they are afflicted in this life, the more they will be consoled in the kingdom of the blessed: "When the cares of my heart are many, your consolations cheer my soul" (Ps 94:19).

For the consolation of desolate souls, I would like to add here what we are told about the life of Saint Jane Frances de Chantal. Over the space of forty-one years she was afflicted by the most dreadful interior trials, by temptations, by fears of being shut out from God's grace, and of being abandoned by him.[24] Her afflictions were so great and unremitting that she went so far as to say that the only relief she had came from the thought of death.[25] Moreover she said: "The attacks are so furious that I don't know where to shelter my poor spirit. At times my patience seems to have deserted me, and I am on the point of losing and leaving behind everything."[26] She adds: "The tyranny of temptation is so cruel that at any time of day I would gladly trade it for the loss of my life; sometimes it happens that I can neither eat nor sleep."[27]

28 • During the last eight or nine years of her life, her temptations became still more savage.[28] Mother de Scatel said that her saintly Mother de Chantal suffered a continuous inner martyrdom night and day, when she prayed, at work, and even during sleep, so that she felt deep compassion for her.[29] The saint endured assaults against all the virtues (except chastity),[30] with violent outbreaks of doubts, darkness, and revulsion.[31] Sometimes God would take away all lights from her, and seem angry with her, as if he were just on the point of driving her away from him. Out of sheer terror, she had to look off in some other direction for relief. But, failing to find any, she was obliged to return to look on God, and to abandon herself to his mercy. At every moment she felt she must collapse under the onslaught of the temptations. God's help did not, in fact, forsake her; but she thought that God had already abandoned her,[32] since she no longer felt any satisfaction, but only boredom, in prayer, in reading spiritual books, in Communion, and in all the other spiritual exercises.[33] Her sole guidance in this state of dereliction was simply to look at her God, and to let him take over.[34]

29 • The saint said: "In all my times of abandonment my simple way is a new cross to me, and my inability to act adds new weight to this cross." And so she said that she felt like a sick person overwhelmed with sufferings, unable to turn from one side to the other, mute, incapable of explaining her troubles, and blind, unable to tell whether the attendants were giving her medicine or poison. And then, bursting into tears, she added, "I seem to be without faith, without hope, and without love for my God."[35] Still, throughout all this, the saint maintained a serene expression and a gentle amiability in conversation, and kept her eyes fixed on God, resting in the bosom of the divine Will. Saint Francis de Sales, who was her director and knew well how beloved her beautiful soul was to almighty God, wrote of her: "Her heart was like a deaf musician, who though he sang wonderfully, could derive no pleasure from it."[36] And to herself he wrote as follows: "You must serve your Savior only for love of his will, utterly deprived of consolations, and flooded with sadness and fear."[37] That is how saints are made.

Polished by the salutary strokes of the chisel
And much pounding by the mason's hammer,

The stones build up this massive structure,
Bound together with proper joints,
And are set at the summit.[38]

The saints are these chosen stones, as the Church sings, carved by strokes of the chisel, that is, by temptations, fears, darkness, and other pains, both inner and outer, thereby making themselves fit to be seated on thrones in the blessed kingdom of Paradise.

Prayers of Love and Affection

Jesus, my hope, my love, and the only love of my soul, I do not deserve your consolations and sweet intimacies; keep them for those innocent souls who have always loved you. Sinner that I am, I do not deserve them, nor do I ask for them. The only thing I seek from you is this: make me love you, make me carry out your will throughout my life; and then dispose of me as you please.

Poor me, I should have to go through an altogether different kind of darkness, terrors, and abandonments for the wrongs I have done you. Hell should have been my fate, where, separated from you forever, and completely abandoned by you, I should have to weep eternally, without being able to love you anymore. No, my Jesus, I accept every punishment, but not this one. You deserve an infinite love; you have too greatly obliged me to love you. No, I do not dare to live and not love you.

I do love you, my sovereign good; I love you with all my heart; I love you more than myself; I love you, and I want to do nothing but love you.

I see that this good will of mine is entirely the gift of your grace; but, my Lord, finish the work, help me always until I die. Do not leave me in my own hands; give me strength to overcome temptations and to conquer myself; and so make me always commend myself to you.

I want to be all yours; I give you my body, my soul, my will, and my freedom; I no longer want to live for myself, but only for you, my Creator, my Redeemer my love, my everything: *My God, and my all.* I want to become a saint, and I hope for this from you.

Afflict me as you will, deprive me of everything, so long as you do not deprive me of your grace and your love.

O Mary, hope of sinners, you are so powerful with God; I greatly trust in your intercession. I beg you by your love for Jesus Christ, help me, and make me a saint.

Farewell, creatures, happily I leave you,
No longer am I yours, nor even mine anymore;
Now freed from everything, my dear Jesus,
My beloved, accept me.

Lovable Lord, let your holy love
Come possess me completely:
Let it reign and rule in this heart of mine
That for an unhappy time rebelled against you.
Lovable Lord, possess me.

O divine love that makes happy
The souls you ignite with heavenly flames,
Oh, come to my heart, and make it worthy
Of your pure love, set it on fire,
Ah, divine love, consume me.

Summary

Of the Virtues Treated in This Work That Must Be Practiced by Those Who Love Jesus Christ

1 • We must patiently endure all the tribulations of this life, the sicknesses, sorrows, poverty, loss of possessions, death of kin, affronts, persecutions, and adversity of every kind. Let us understand that the sufferings of this life are signs that God loves us, and show his desire to save us in the next. Moreover, we must realize that the involuntary mortifications that God himself sends us are more pleasing to him than the voluntary ones that we take up on our own.

2 • In sickness let us try to resign ourselves completely to the will of God, which pleases him more than any other devotion. If at such times we cannot apply our minds to meditation, let us look at the Crucified, offering him our sufferings and uniting them to those that he endured for us upon the cross. And when we are told of our approaching death, let us accept the news in peace and in the spirit of sacrifice, that is, with the willingness to die so as to give pleasure to Jesus Christ: it was this desire that gave all the merit to the death of the martyrs. Then we must say: "Lord, here I am, I want everything that you want." And let us not go looking for more life, in order

to do penance for our sins. Accepting death with complete resignation is worth more than any penance.

3 • In addition we must practice conformity to the will of God in bearing poverty and all the troubles and inconveniences that poverty brings with it: cold, hunger, fatigue, disgrace, and scorn.

4 • We should likewise be resigned to the loss of property as well as the loss of relatives and friends, who while they were alive could do us good. Whenever we meet with adversity, let us get used to saying: God wanted it this way, and so do I. And upon the death of family members, instead of wasting time in pointless tears, let us use it to pray for their souls, and offer up to Jesus Christ the pain we feel at having lost them.

5 • Furthermore, we must force ourselves to endure scorn and insults in peace and tranquillity. To those who abuse us, let us respond with gentle words; but as long as we feel upset, it is better to keep silent, until the mind settles down. In the meantime let us take care not to complain to others about the affront we have received, but offer it up in silence to Jesus Christ, who endured so many things for us.

6 • We should behave kindly to all, superiors and inferiors, nobles and plebeians, relatives and strangers; but especially to the poor and sick, and, above all, to those who regard us with hostility.

7 • In reproving the faults of others, gentleness is more effective than any other means or reason. Hence we should beware of correcting anyone when we are angry, because then the correction will always turn out bitter, either in language or manner. Beware, too, of correcting the wrongdoer when he is angry; because then the correction will be more likely to exasperate him than to make him mend his ways.

8 • We are not to envy the great ones of this world the riches, honors, dignities, and applause that they receive from others. We should rather envy those who most love Jesus Christ, for they undoubtedly live more happily than the greatest monarchs on earth. Thank the Lord for enlightening you by showing you the vanity of all worldly goods, for which so many wretches are lost.

9 • In all our actions and thoughts we should not seek our own satisfaction, but only the pleasure of God; and so we shouldn't be disturbed when some of our plans fail. When they succeed, we should not seek the applause and thanks of others. If they speak ill of us, we should pay no heed, consoling ourselves with the thought that we acted to please God, not human beings.

10 • The chief means of perfection are (1) to avoid all deliberate sin, however slight. But if we have the misfortune to commit some fault, let us be careful not to become angry and impatient with ourselves. In that case we must quietly repent, and while making an act of love for Jesus Christ, promise, with his help, never to do it again.

11 • (2) To desire to reach the perfection of the saints, and to suffer anything to please Jesus Christ; and if we do not have this desire, to pray to Jesus Christ, in his goodness, to give it to us; because otherwise, if we do not sincerely desire to become saints, we shall never take a single step forward on the way of perfection.

12 • (3) To have a firm resolve to reach perfection. Those who lack such resolution work only with feeble energy, and when put to the test they cannot overcome their repugnances. By contrast resolute souls, with God's unfailing help, overcome every obstacle.

13 • (4) To spend two hours, or at least one hour, each day in mental prayer; and, unless strictly necessary, never to abandon it, regardless of the boredom, dryness, or unrest that we may feel.

14 • (5) To take holy Communion several times a week, depending on the advice of our spiritual director. The same rule holds good with regard to external mortifications, such as fasting, wearing a hair shirt, whipping oneself, and the like. Mortifications of this kind, unless carried out under the supervision of a spiritual director, will either destroy our health or make us proud. Hence one must have a spiritual director, so that everything may proceed under the rule of obedience.

15 • (6) To pray continuously, commending ourselves to Jesus Christ for all our needs, having recourse as well to the intercession of our guardian angel, of our patron saints, and most particularly of the Mother of God, through whose hands God grants us all graces.

It has already been shown, toward the end of Chapter VIII, that all our well-being depends on prayer. In particular we must beg God every day for perseverance in his grace. Everyone who asks for perseverance obtains it, but those who do not ask for it do not obtain it and are damned. We must pray to Jesus Christ for his holy love and perfect conformity to his will. And we must seek all graces through the merits of Jesus Christ. We should say these prayers when we rise in the morning, and then repeat them during our meditation, at Communion, during visits to the Blessed Sacrament, and in the evening when we make our examination of conscience. Above all we must ask for God's help in resisting temptation, especially temptations against purity, when we should call again and again on the holy names of Jesus and Mary. Those who pray conquer; those who do not pray are conquered.

16 • With respect to humility, we should not become vain over our riches, honors, high birth, talents, or any other natural advantage, and still less over any spiritual quality, since all are the gifts of God. We should consider ourselves the worst of all, and consequently find satisfaction in being despised by others; and not act as some do, who say they are the worst of all, and then want to be treated as the best. So we should accept reprimands humbly, without trying to excuse ourselves, even when falsely accused; except when defending ourselves is necessary in order to avoid giving scandal to others.

17 • Still more we ought to beware of the desire to show off in the world and to be honored by others. We should never lose sight of the maxim of Saint Francis: "We are what we are in God's eyes, nothing more."[1] It would be still worse for a religious to seek posts of honor and superiority in the community. The true honor of a religious is to be the most humble of all; and those are the humblest of all who most joyfully embrace humiliations.

18 • We must detach our hearts from all creatures. Those who are attached to anything in this world, even the slightest, will never be able to take flight and reach complete union with God.

19 • We must especially detach ourselves from affection for our relatives. Saint Philip Neri said that, "Whatever we invest in affection for creatures is so much taken away from God."[2] In choosing a state of life, we must be particularly on our guard against parents and relatives, who are looking out for their own interests rather than our welfare. We must break away from fear of what people will say and, above all, be detached from self-will. We must abandon everything in order to gain everything. "All for all," writes Thomas à Kempis.[3]

20 • We must never get angry, regardless of what happens. But, if at any time, we find ourselves surprised by anger, then we should immediately commend ourselves to God and refrain from acting or speaking until we are sure that the anger has subsided. Hence it is useful to make ourselves ready in prayer for any sort of conflict that may befall us, so that if it does happen, we may not take offense in a culpable way. We should remember what Saint Francis de Sales admitted about himself: "I have never taken offense without regretting it afterwards."[4]

21 • All holiness consists in loving God, and all love of God consists in doing his will. We must, therefore, resign ourselves without reservation to whatever God decides to do with us, and so peacefully embrace whatever forms of adversity or prosperity God wants for us, whatever state of life God wants for us, whatever kind of health God wants for us. And this should be the aim of all our prayers, that God make us carry out his holy will. And in order to be sure of what God wants, religious must obey their superiors, and laypeople their confessors. Both should rely on what Saint Philip Neri said: "We are not accountable to God for anything done out of obedience"—apart, of course, from actions that are evidently sinful.[5]

22 • There are two remedies against temptations: resignation and prayer. Resignation because, although temptations to sin do not come from God, he permits them for our good. Hence let us beware of becoming angry, however annoying the temptations may be. Let us resign ourselves to the will of God, who permits temptations, and take up arms to overcome them with prayer, the strongest and surest weapon for defeating our enemies.

Evil thoughts, however filthy and wicked, are not sins; only consenting to evil is sinful. So long as we call on the holy names of Jesus and Mary we shall never be conquered. When temptation attacks, it helps to renew our resolution to die rather than to offend God. It is also useful to make the sign of the cross several times and with holy water. It is a great help, too, to tell one's confessor about the temptation. But the most necessary remedy is prayer, asking Jesus and Mary for help in resisting it.

23 • When in spiritual desolation, there are two acts in which we ought particularly to exercise ourselves: (1) to humble ourselves by confessing that we deserve to be treated this way; (2) to resign ourselves to the will of God, and to throw ourselves into the arms of his divine goodness. When God consoles us, let us prepare ourselves for the tribulations that usually come in the wake of consolation. Then when he brings us into desolation, let us be humble and resigned to God's will, and we will derive much more profit from desolation than from consolation.

24 • In order to live well at all times, we must imprint on our minds certain general maxims of eternal life:

Everything in this life comes to an end, both joys and sorrows; but eternity never ends.

At the moment of death, what good is all worldly greatness?

Whatever comes from God, whether it be prosperity or adversity, is good and for our welfare.

We must abandon everything to gain everything.

Without God there can be no true peace.

The only thing necessary is to love God and save one's soul.

The only thing we need to fear is sin.

If God is lost, all is lost,

Those who desire nothing from this world are masters of the whole world.

Those who pray are saved, those who do not are damned.

Let me die and give God pleasure.

Whatever God costs, the price can never be too high.

For those who have deserved hell, all pains are trifles.

Those who look on Jesus crucified will endure anything.

Everything not done entirely for God turns into sorrow.

Those who want God alone are rich in every way.

Happy are those who can say from the heart: "My Jesus I want you alone, and nothing more."

Those who love God will find pleasure in everything; those who do not love God will never find true pleasure in anything.

Notes

Introduction

1. Historical Institute of the Redemptorists, *Studia et subsidia de vita et operibus S. Alfonsi Mariae de Ligoria* (1696–1787) Rome: Collegio S. Alfonso, 1990), 485–534, 565–570.
2. Kevin O'Shea, C.Ss.R, *The Courtesy of God,* [a paper delivered at the Catholic Institute of Sydney, ——, NSW].
3. See Chapter VII, #33 to #38 of *The Practice of the Love of Jesus Christ.*
4. Ibid. See Chapter XIII.
5. See Alphonsus M. de Liguori, *The Great Means of Salvation and Perfection,* Part II, Section VI.
6. Alphonsus M. Liguori, *Homo Apostolicus,* Book III, Chapter I, #2, paragraph 6.
7. See Chapter IV, #12, of *The Practice of the Love of Jesus Christ.*

Chapter I

1. Jean-Pierre Camus, *Esprit de S. François de Sales*, part 1, ch. 1; Saint Francis de Sales, *Introduction to the Devout Life*, part 1, ch. 1.
2. Saint Augustine, *In Epistolam Ioannis ad Parthos*, treatise 7, n. 8, ML 35–2033.
3. *Officium S. Agnetis*, Jan. 21, Nocturn I, antiphon 1.
4. Saint Augustine, *Confessions*, book 10, ch. 6, n. 8, ML 32–782.
5. Dom A. J. Le Bouthillier de Rancé, Abbé de la Trappe, *De la sainteté et des devoirs de la vie monastique*, ch. 7, vol. 1.
6. Vincenzo Puccini, *Vita* [of Saint Mary Magdalen de Pazzi], (Florence, 1611), part 1, ch. 34.
7. Saint Teresa of Ávila, *The Life of the Holy Mother Teresa of Jesus,* ch. 9 in *Complete Works*, edited by E. Allison Peers (New York: Sheed and Ward, 1963).
8. Giambattista Scaramelli, *Direttorio Ascetico*, treatise 1, art. 7, ch. 4, n. 201. The devout hermit Alphonsus speaks of is Saint Simeon Salo.
9. Saint Francis de Sales, *Traité de l'amour de Dieu*, book 7, ch. 8.
10. Ibid. and book 12, ch. 13.
11. *Tractatus de caritate*, ch. 6, n. 29 in *Opera S. Bernardi*, ML 184–599; Saint Bernard, *In Cantica, Sermo* 64, n. 10, ML 183–1088.
12. Isidoro Toscano di Paola, *Vita* (Venice, 1691), book 4, ch. 7.
13. Saint Laurence Giustiniani, *Sermo in Nativitate Domini*, n. 4, *Opera* (Lyon, 1628), p. 394.
14. Puccini, *Vita*, part I, ch. 11.
15. Dionysius Areopagita, *De divinis nominibus,* ch. 4, §13, MG 3–711.

16. Gallizia, *Vita*, book 6, ch. 2 (end): *Massime e detti spirituali, Massime per gli ecclesiastici*, n. 5.
17. Bonaventure, *Stimulus amoris*, part 1, ch. 1.
18. Blessed John of Ávila, *Trattati del SS. Sacramento dell'Eucaristia*, treatise I: *Sopra l'amor di Dio verso gli uomini*, nn. 14–18.
19. Johannes Tauler, O. P., *Epistola 20: Sermones de festis, Institutiones, cum Epistolis aliquot* (Lyon, 1558).
20. Bonaventure, *Stimulus amoris*, part 1, ch. 1.
21. Bernardinus de Bustis, O. M., *Rosarium sermonum per Quadragesimam*, part 2, sermon 15; *Feria VI in Parasceven, de lacrimosa Passione Domini*.
22. Bonaventure, *Legenda S. Francisci*, ch. 8, n. 6; ch. 13, n. 3; Luke Wadding, *Annales Minorum*, for the year 1208, n. 12.
23. Giorgio Tiepolo, *Le considerazioni della Passione di N.S. Gesu* Cristo (Venice, 1618), treatise 10, meditation 37.

Chapter II

1. Saint Bernardine of Siena, O. M., *Quadrageimale de Evangelio aeterno*, sermon 54, *in Coena Domini*, art. 1, ch. 1, *Opera* (Venice, 1745), vol. 2.
2. Saint John Chrysostom, *Expositio in Ps. 44*, n. 11, MG 55–200.
3. Concilium Tridentinum, *Sessio* 13, *Decretum de SS. Eucharistiae Sacramento*, ch. 2.
4. Bernardine of Siena, *Quadragesimale de Evangelio aeterno*, sermon 54, *in Coena Domini*, art. 1, ch. 1.
5. Saint Thomas Aquinas, *Summa Theologica*, part 3, ques. 73, art. 3, *ad* 3; and part 3, ques. 78, art. 3, *ad* 6.
6. In *Opera S. Bernardi* (author unknown), *Sermo de excellentia SS. Sacramenti et dignitate sacerdotum*, n. 10, ML 184–987.
7. *Officium Corporis Domini*, antiphon for the *Magnificat*, second Vespers.
8. Pietro Giacomo Bacci, of the Oratory, *Vita* [of Saint Philip Neri], (expanded edition after the canonization), (Brescia, 1706), book 4, ch. 1, n. 4.
9. Isaiah 12:4.
10. Saint Augustine, *Enarratio in Ps. XXXIII*, sermon 1, n. 8, ML 36–305.
11. Saint Laurence Giustiniani, *De triumphali agone Mediatoris Christi, Opera* (Lyon, 1628), p. 278.
12. Dionysius Aeropagita, *De divinis nominibus*, ch. 4, §15, MG 3–714.
13. Thomas Aquinas, *Summa Theologica*, part I–II, ques. 28, art. 1, *ad* 2.
14. Saint Francis de Sales, *Introduction to the Devout Life*, part 2, ch. 21.
15. Saint John Chrysostom, *Ad populum Antiochenum*, homily 61, *in Ionnem*, MG 59–260.
16. Saint Laurence Giustiniani, *De incendio divini amoris*, ch. 5, *Opera* (Lyon, 1628), p. 740.
17. Bernardine of Siena, *Quadragesimale de Evangelio eterno*, sermon 54, *in Coena Domini*, art. 4, ch. 1.
18. P. H. Choquet, O. P., *Vitae*, pp. 144–200.

19. Francis de Sales, *Introduction to the Devout Life,* part 2, ch. 21.
20. Dionysius Aeropagita, *De ecclesiastica hierarchia*, ch. 3, I, MG 3–423.
21. Saint Vincent Ferrer, *Sermones aestivales* (Venice, 1573), *In die sancto Paschae*, sermon 2, folio 7, from the back.
22. Concilium Tridentinium, *Sessio* 13, *Decretum de SS. Eucharistiae Sacramento*, ch. 2.
23. Thomas Aquinas, *Summa Theologica*, III, ques. 79, art. 4.
24. Innocent III, *De sacro Altaris mysterio libre sex,* book 4, ch. 44, ML 217–885.
25. Raymond of Capua, O. P., *Vita*, part 2, ch. 6.
26. Leonardus Hansen, O. P., *Vita* (Rome, 1664) ch. 22.
27. Bollandists, *Acta Sanctorum*, September 28.
28. Saint John Chrysostom, *De Poenitentia*, homily 9, MG 49–345; *In Ioannem*, homily 46 (45), n. 3, MG 59–260, 261.
29. Saint Gregory of Nyssa, *In Cantica Canticorum*, homily 4, MG 44–846.
30. Jean de Gerson, *Collectorium super Magnificat*, treatise 9, section 3. *Opera* (Antwerp, 1706), vol. 3; *Tractatus de praeparatione ad missam,* consideration 4, *Opera*, vol. 3.
31. Saint Bonaventure, *De profectu Religiosorum*, in *Opera S. Bonaventurae* (Lyon, 1668), vol. 7, p. 612.
32. Francis de Sales, *Introduction to the Devout Life*, part 2, ch. 21.
33. Lud. Blosius, O. S. B., Abbas Latiensis in Hannonnia, *Conclave animae fidelis*, part 2, or *Monile spirituale*, ch. 6, n.6.

Chapter III

1. Saint Thomas of Villanova, *Conciones*, vol. 1: in Dom. I Adventus, concio 5, n. 13.
2. Saint Teresa of Ávila, *The Life of the Holy Mother Teresa of Jesus,* ch. 25., in *Complete Works*, edited by E. Allison Peers (New York: Sheed and Ward, 1963).
3. Ibid., ch. 8.
4. Saint Bonaventure, *De triplici via*, ch. 2, §2, n. 3; *Opera*, vol. 8 (ad Claras Aquas, 1898), p. 8.
5. Saint Leo the Great, *Sermo 73* (71) *de Ascensione Domini* primus.
6. Blessed John of Ávila, *Lettere spirituali* (Rome, 1669), part 2; *Ad una donna...turbata assai, parendole star lontana dal Signore.* These letters correspond to the following numbers: 11, 12, 13, 14, 15. The final section (n. 15) is taken not from the *Lettere*, but from the *Trattati del SS. Sacramento dell'Eucaristia* (Rome, 1608), treatise 8.

Chapter IV

1. Saint Bernard, *In Cantica*, sermon 83, n. 4, ML 183–1183.
2. Saint Francis de Sales, *Traité de l'amour de Dieu,* book 7, ch. 8.
3. Office for the feast of Corpus Christi, antiphon for the *Magnificat*, second Vespers.

4. Francis de Sales, *Traité de l'amour de Dieu,* book 12, ch. 13.
5. Saint Thomas of Villanova, *In Dominicam XVII post Pentecosten,* concio 3, n. 7.
6. Bernard, *In Cantica*, sermon 61, n. 4, ML 183–1072.
7. *Vie du Pere Jean Rigoleu, S. J.* (d. 1658) (Lyon, 1739), 4th ed., p. 62.
8. Bernard, *In Cantica*, sermon 83, nn. 4–5, ML 183–1183.
9. Saint Thomas Aquinas, *Summa Theologica*, part I–II, ques. 62, *De virtutibus theologicis*, art. 4, c.; part II–II, ques. 23, art. 6, 7, 8.
10. Bernard, *In Cantica,* sermon 71, n. 8, ML 183–1125; *In Cantica*, sermon 8, n. 9, ML 183–814.
11. Saint Augustine, *De moribus Ecclesiae catholicae et de moribus Manichaeorum libri duo*, book 1, ch. 22, nn. 40–41, ML 32–1328, 1329.
12. Augustine, *De bono viduitatis liber*, ch. 21, n. 26, ML 40–448.
13. Saint John Chrysostom, *In Genesim*, homily 55, nn. 2–3, MG 54–481, 482, and homily 34, nn. 5–6, MG 53–319, 320, 321.
14. Jean Pierre Camus, *Esprit de S. François de Sales*, part I, ch. 25, and part 7, ch. 4; and Saint Francis de Sales, *Introduction to the Devout Life*, part 1, ch. 1.
15. Saint Teresa of Ávila, *The Life of the Holy Mother Teresa of Jesus*, ch. 40, in *Complete Works*, edited by E. Allison Peers (New York: Sheed and Ward, 1963).

Chapter V

1. Saint Augustine, in the appendix to *Sermones S. Augustini*, sermon 52, n. 4, ML 39–1845.
2. Augustine, *The City of God*, book 1, ch. 8, n. 2, ML 41–21; *Sermo* 252, ch. 5, n. 5, ML 38–1174, 1175.
3. Saint Teresa of Ávila, *Mercedes de Dios*, XXXVI; *Obras*, book 2, 64, 65.
4. Teresa of Ávila, *The Conceptions of the Love of God*, ch. 6, in *The Complete Works*, edited by E. Allison Peers (New York: Sheed and Ward, 1963).
5. Teresa of Ávila, *Declaración de la Hermana* in *Obras*, book 2, appendix 57.
6. Louis Abelly (bishop of Rodez), *Vie* [of Saint Vincent de Paul] (1881) book 3, ch. 22.
7. Bartolomeo da Pisa, *De conformitate vitae B. Francisci ad vitam Domini Iesu Christi Redemptoris nostri*, (Milan, 1513), folio 28, col. 2.
8. Saint John Chrysostom, *In Episit. ad Philip.*, homily 4, n. 3, MG 62–208, 209; *In Epist. ad Ephes.*, homily 8, n. 1, MG 62–55, 56, 57; *Ad pop. Antioch.*, homily 16, n. 3, MG 49–164, 165.
9. Gallizia, *Vita*, book 6, ch. 2 (at the end): *Massime e detti spirituali, Massime per gli ecclesiastici*, n. 5.
10. Saint Gregory the Great, *Homiliae XL in Evangelia*, book 2, homily 35, n. 7, ML 76–1263.
11. Teresa of Ávila, *Mercedes de Dios*, XXXVI, *Obras*, book 2, (Burgos, 1915).
12. Teresa of Ávila, *The Way of Perfection,* ch. 18.

13. Teresa of Ávila, *Life*, ch. 11.
14. B. Cimarelli, *Croniche degli Ordini istituiti dal P. S. Francesco*, ed. Leonardo da Napoli, (Naples, 1680), vol. 3, book 4, ch. 24.
15. Teresa of Ávila, *Book of the Foundations*, ch. 31.
16. Bollandists, *Acta Sanctorum*, August 25, ch. 2, n. 23.
17. Luke Wadding, *Annales Minorum*, for the yeat 1227, n. 8.
18. P. Talenti, *Vita*, book 6, ch. 2, pp. 481–482.
19. Bollandists, *Acta S. Agapiti*, n. 4; *Acta Sanctorum*, August 18.
20. Saint Francis of Assisi, *The Little Flowers of Saint Francis: On the Most Holy Stigmata of Saint Francis*, consideration 1.
21. Pietro Giacomo Bacci, *Vita*, (Brescia, 1706), book 2, ch. 20, n. 20.
22. Teresa of Ávila, *The Conceptions of the Love of God*, ch. 2.
23. Saint Francis de Sales, Letter 540 to Baron de Chantal, July 14, 1609 (1615), *Oeuvres* (Annecy, 1906), vol. 14.
24. *Alcuni avvisi salutari trovati nei manoscritti del P. da Ponte*, n. 4; Longara Degli Oddi, S. J., *Vita* (Rome, 1761), last chapter.
25. Galluzzi, S. J., *Vita del P. Paolo Segneri Juniore*, (Rome, 1716), book 4, ch. 2.
26. Teresa of Ávila, *Life*, ch. 10.
27. D. Bartoli, *Vita*, book 4, ch. 37: *Detti de S. Ignazio.*
28. Saint Gertrude, O. S. B., *Legatus divinae pietatis*, book 4, ch. 15, (Solesmes edition, 1875).
29. G. B. Pacichelli, *Vita della Ven. Suor Maria Vittoria Angelini*, Romana, Terziaria dell'Ord. de' Servi (1590–1659), part 3, p. 495, *Lettera alla Badessa di Sant'Oreste.*
30. Blessed John of Ávila, *Lettere spirituali*, (Rome, 1669), part 1, letter 41, p. 208.
31. Blessed Angela Foligno, *Vita et Opuscula* (Foligno, 1714), book II; *Opuscula B. Angelae*, part 3: *De triplici virtute et de amore divino*; ch. 4: *De via, conditione et signis amoris.*
32. Vincenzo Puccini, *Vita* [of Mary Magdalen de Pazzi], (Florence, 1611), part 1, ch. 47.
33. C. Marabotto and E. Vernazza, *Vita* [of Saint Catherine of Genoa], ch. 29.
34. Saint John of the Cross, *Opere*, (Venice, 1769), vol. 1, *Salita del Monte Carmelo*, book 2, ch. 6.
35. Francis de Sales, *Les vrais Entretiens spirituels: Oeuvres*, (Annecy, 1895), vol. VI, appendix II, D, pp. 447–448.
36. Teresa of Ávila, *The Way of Perfection*, ch. 36.
37. Puccini, *Vita*, (Padua, 1671), ch. 83.
38. Tommaso Campora, S. J., *Vita*, book 2, ch. 12.
39. John Chrysostom, *In Ioannem*, homily 88 (87), n. 3, MG 59–476; *In Epist. ad Rom.*, homily 9, n. 4, MG 60–474; *In Genesim*, ch. 9, homily 28, nn. 3–6, MG 53–256, 259, 260; *Expositio in Ps. 41*, n. 5, MG 55–163.

Chapter VI

1. Saint Francis de Sales, Letter 1539, July–August, 1619, to Madame de Villesavin, *Oeuvres*, XVIII, 417.
2. Francis de Sales, Letter 1254, November 10, 1616, to Madame Guillet de Monthoux, *Oeuvres*, XVIII, 305–306.
3. Francis de Sales, Letter 1223, July 22, 1616, to Mère de Bréchard, *Oeuvres*, XVII, 260.
4. Saint Jane Frances de Chantal, *Déposition pour la béatification et canonisation de S. François* (Procès d'Annecy, 1627), art. 32, *Vie et Oeuvres de la Sainte*, III, 167.
5. Louis Abelly, *Vie* [of Saint Vincent de Paul], book 3, ch. 12 (27).
6. Jane Frances de Chantal, *Déposition pour la béatification et canonisation de S. François*, art. 27, *Vie et Oeuvres de la Sainte*, III, 130.
7. Francis de Sales, *Introduction to the Devout Life*, part 3, ch. 8.
8. Jean-Pierre Camus (abridged edition by Collet), *Esprit de S. François de Sales*, part 5, ch. 10.
9. Abelly, *Vie*, book 3, ch. 24, section 1.
10. Mére de Chaugy, *Mémoires sur la vie et les vertus de S. Jeanne de Chantal*, part 3, ch. 19, *Vie et Oeuvres de la Sainte*, I, p. 466.
11. Francis de Sales, *Introduction to the Devout Life*, part 3, ch. 8.
12. Surio, *De probatis sanctorum historiis*, October 10, *Vita S. Ioannis* (prior of the monastery of Bridlington).
13. Camus, *Esprit de S. François de Sales* (abridged ed.), part 1, ch. 3; Letter 2090 (fragments), to Mère de Chantal, 1615–1617, *Oeuvres*, XXI, 176.
14. Abelly, *Vie*, book 3, ch. 12.
15. Camus, *Esprit de S. François de Sales*, part 3, ch. 11, 21; part 5, ch. 11; part 10, ch. 2, 4, 5; part 14, ch. 13.
16. Abelly, *Vie*, book 3, ch. 12.
17. Acami, of the Oratory of Rome, *Vita*, (Rome, 1677), book 1, ch. 11.
18. Saint Bernard, *De adventu Domini*, sermon 4, n. 5, ML 183–49.
19. Pier Matteo Petrucci, biship of Jesi (1681), cardinal (1686), d. 1701, *Poesie sacre, morali e spirituali*, (Jesi, 1685), p. 143.
20. Francis de Sales, Letter 540, July 14 (probably 1609), to Baron de Chantal, *Oeuvres*, XIV, 177, 178.
21. Saint Teresa of Ávila, *The Life of the Holy Mother Teresa of Jesus*, ch. 30, in *The Complete Works*, edited by E. Allison Peers (New York: Sheed and Ward, 1963).
22. Saint Aloysius Gonzaga, *Vita* (Cepari), part 2, ch. 7, ch. 8.
23. C. Marabotti and E. Vernazza, *Vita* [of Saint Catherine of Genoa], ch. 16.

Chapter VII

1. Saint Gregory the Great, *Moralia in Job,* book 10, ch. 6 (8).
2. Saint Paulinus (bishop of Nola), *Epistola 38*, ad Aprum, n. 6, ML 61–360.
3. Vincenzo Puccini, *Vita* [of Mary Magdelen de Pazzi], part 1, ch. 58.
4. This religious must be Father Francesco M. Margotta.
5. Blessed John of Ávila, *Lettera a una persona che desiderava servire a Dio, ma non le bastava l'animo: Lettere spirituali*, (Rome, 1669), part 1, letter 30.
6. Saint John Chrysostom, *De compunctione,* book 2, ad Stelechium, n. 6, MG 47–420.
7. Saint Teresa of Ávila, *The Book of the Foundations*, ch. 5 in *The Complete Works* edited by E. Allison Peers (New York: Sheed and Ward, 1963).
8. Ibid., ch. 12.
9. Puccini, *Vita*, 1671, ch. 107.
10. J. B. Saint Jure, S. J., *De la connaissance et de l'amour de Fils de Dieu Notre–Seigneur Jésus–Christ*, book 3, ch. 15 (book 3, part 2, ch. 3).
11. L. da Ponte, *Vita* [of Baltasar Álvarez], ch. 2, §1, and ch. 49.

Chapter VIII

1. Saint Gregory the Great, *Moralia in Job*, book 10, ch. 6 (8), n. 10.
2. Saint Francis de Sales, Letter 280, April, 1605, to Madame Bourgeois, *Oeuvres,* (Annecy, 1904), XIII.
3. Francis de Sales, Letter 1382, to Madame de la Valbonne, *Oeuvres*, XVIII (Annecy, 1912). See Jean-Pierre Camus, *Esprit de S. François de Sales,* part 15, ch. 8.
4. G. Turano, *Vita...della Ven...Suor Maria Crocifissa della Concezione, O. S. B.*, nel Monastero de Palma, book 1, ch. 10.
5. Concilium Tridentinum, *Sessio* 13, *Decretum de SS. Eucharistiae Sacramento*, ch. 2.
6. Saint Teresa of Ávila, *The Way of Perfection*, ch. 41, in *The Complete Works,* edited by E. Allison Peers (New York: Sheed and Ward, 1963).
7. Teresa of Ávila, *Interior Castle: Fifth Mansions*, ch. 3.
8. Teresa of Ávila, *The Book of the Foundations*, ch. 29.
9. Saint Gregory the Great, *Regulae pastoralis liber,* part 3, ch. 34 (58), at the end, ML 77–119.
10. Patrignani, *Menologio di pie memorie d'alcuni Religiosi d. C. d. G.*, February 16, 1624.
11. Saint Bonaventure, *Legenda S. Francisi*, ch. 5, n. 5, *Opera* (ad Claras Aquas, 1898), vol. 8, p. 517; Marco da Lisbona, *Croniche del P. S. Francesco*, book 1, ch. 33; *Opuscula B. P. Francisci* (Pedeponti, 1739), p. 44: *Collatio* 6.
12. Saint Laurence Giustiniani, *De disciplina et perfectione monasticae conversationis*, ch. 6, *Opera* (Lyon, 1628), p. 90.
13. Saint Augustine, *Epistola seu liber ad Demetriadem*, ch. 27, *Opera S. Augustini,* ML 33–1118.
14. Teresa of Ávila, *The Conceptions of the Love of God,* ch. 2.

15. Teresa of Ávila, *The Life of the Holy Mother Teresa of Jesus*, ch. 39, in *The Complete Works*, edited by E. Allison Peers (New York: Sheed and Ward, 1963).
16. Ibid.
17. Cf. Teresa of Ávila, *The Way of Perfection*, ch. 34; *Life*, ch. 22.
18. Teresa of Ávila, *Life*, ch. 13.
19. Vincenzo Puccini, *Vita* [of Saint Mary Magdalen de Pazzi] (Florence, 1611), part 3, *Giorno secondo*, pp. 46–47.
20. Francis de Sales, *Introduction to the Devout Life*, part 3, ch. 37.
21. Teresa of Ávila, *The Book Called the Foundations*, ch. 28; *The Way of Perfection*, ch. 23.
22. Teresa of Ávila, *Life*, ch. 39.
23. Ibid., ch. 4.
24. Francis de Sales, Letter 2092, *à Mère de Chantal*, from the years 1615–1622, *Oeuvres* (Annecy, 1923), XXI.
25. Francis de Sales, *Introduction to the Devout Life*, book 12, ch. 8.
26. G. M. Magenis, *Vita*, (Brescia, 1739), book 1, ch. 8, *Appendice storica*.
27. Saint Laurence Gustiniani, *De disciplina et perfectione monasticae conversationis*, ch. 6, 24, *Opera* (Lugundi, 1628)
28. Nicholas Lancisio, S. J., *Opuscula spiritualia* (Ingolstadt, 1724), vol. 1: *Opusculum spirituale*, VI, ch. 22.
29. Giussano, *De fama, virtutibus et miraculis S. Caroli Borromaei*, book 1, (*Vita*, book 8), ch. 26.
30. Saint Alphonsus attributes this saying to Saint Bernard, but it comes from Saint Bonaventure, *De informatione novitiorum*, part 2, ch. 3.
31. Teresa of Ávila, *Life*, ch. 11.
32. Ibid., ch. 39.
33. Saint John Chrysostom, *In Matthaeum*, homily 25 (26), n. 3, MG 57–331, 332.
34. Jean de Gerson, *Tractatulus consolatorius de meditatione*, consideration 7, *Opera* (Antwerp, 1706), vol. 3.
35. Teresa of Ávila, *Obras*, IX, p. 280.
36. Saint Bernard, *De consideratione* ad Eugenium, III, book 1, ch. 2, n. 3, ML 182–730.
37. Ibid., book 1, ch. 7, ML 182–737.
38. G. Turano, *Vita... della Ven... Suor Maria Crocifissa della Concezione, O. S. B., nel Monastero de Palma*, book 2, ch. 8.
39. Teresa of Ávila, *Interior Castle: First Mansions*, ch. 1. But see Palladio, *Historia Lausiaca (De vitis Patrum*, book 3, ch. 98), ML 73–1190.
40. G. Grassetti, S. J., *Vita della beata Caterina da Bologna* (Bologna, 1724), book 3, ch. 2.
41. Teresa of Ávila, *Life*, ch. 8.
42. Ibid., ch. 19.
43. Ibid.
44. Cepari, *Vita* [of Saint Aloysius of Gonzaga], book 2, ch. 7.

45. Lodovico Sabbatini d'Anfora, *Vita del Padre D. Antonio de Torres*, Preposito Gen. della Cong. de' Pii Operai (Naples, 1732), book 4, ch. 1, pp. 290–291.
46. Teresa of Ávila, *Life*, ch. 19.
47. Teresa of Ávila, *The Book of the Foundations*, ch. 5.
48. Teresa of Ávila, *Life*, ch. 34.
49. Barth. Povius, *Vita*, book 7, §6.
50. Teresa of Ávila, Letter 8 to D. Alfonso Velásquez, with annotations by Giovanni de Palafox y Mendoza, n. 10 (Venice, 1739). (This letter is apocryphal.)
51. Francis de Sales, *Traité de l'amour de Dieu*, book 12, ch. 13, *Oeuvres* (Annecy, 1894), V, 346.
52. Teresa of Ávila, *The Way of Perfection*, ch. 34.
53. *Decretum S. C. Concilii circa communionem quotidianam*, February 12, 1679; *Fontes Juris Canonici*, vol. V, n. 2848.
54. *Sessio* 13, *Decretum de SS. Eucharistiae Sacramento*, ch. 2.
55. Saint Bernard, *Sermo in Coena Domino*, n. 3, ML 183–272, 273.
56. Saint Thomas Aquinas, *Summa Theologica*, III, ques. 79, art. 6, c.
57. Saint John Chrysostom, *In Ioannem*, homily 46 (45), nn. 3–4, MG 59–261, 262; *In Matthaeum*, homily 4, n. 9, MG 57–50; *In Epist. I ad Cor.*, homily 24, n. 5, MG 61–204.
58. Blessed John of Ávila, *Trattati del SS. Sacramento Dell' Eucaristia*, treatise 27.
59. Francis de Sales, *Introduction to the Devout Life*, part 2, ch. 20.
60. Thomas Aquinas, *In IV Sententiarum*, distinction XII, ques. 3, art. 1, *Ad secundum quaestionem*.
61. John of Ávila, *Lettere spirituali* (Florence, 1601), part 1, *ad un sacerdote... la vita sua*, p. 77.
62. Vincenzo Puccini, *Vita* [of Saint Mary Magdalen de Pazzi], (Florence, 1611) part 1, ch. 65.
63. Teresa of Ávila, *The Way of Perfection*, ch. 34.
64. Saint Ambrose, *De Sacramentis*, book 4, ch 6, n. 28, ML 16–446.
65. Saint Gregory Nazianzen, *Carminum*, book 1, section 2, XXXIII, *Tetrastichae sententiae*, sententia 37, verses 145–148, MG 37–938, 939.
66. Jean de Gerson, *Collectorium super Magnificat*, treatise 9, part 3, *Opera*, (Antwerp, 1706), book 3.
67. Concilium Tridentinum, *Sessio* 13, *Decretum de SS. Eucharistiae Sacramento*, ch. 8
68. Thomas Aquinas, *Summa Theologica*, III, ques. 80, art 1, *ad* 3.
69. Probably Saint Agata della Croce (d. 1621).
70. Theodoretus, *Religiosa Historia*, ch. 16, MG 84–1418, ML 74–75.
71. Augustine, *Enarratio in Ps. 65*, n. 24, ML 36–801.
72. John Chrysostom, *In Matthaeum*, homily 55 (56), n. 5, MG 58–538, 539.
73. Augustine, *De dono perseverantiae*, ch. 16, n. 39, ML 45–1017.
74. Thomas Aquinas, *Summa Theologica*, III, question 39, art. 5, c.
75. Concilium Tridentinum, *Sessio* 6, *De iustificatione*, ch. 13.
76. Augustine, *De dono perseverantiae*, book 6, ch. 10, ML 45–999.

77. Gregory the Great, *Ps. VI paenitentialis* (Ps. CIX), n. 2, ML 79–633.
78. Puccini, *Vita,* (Florence, 1611), part 3, *Quinta Notte*, pp. 126–127.
79. Augustine, *Enarratio in Ps. 83*, n. 16, ML 37–1445.
80. Thomas Aquinas, *Summa Theologica*, II–II, question 178, art. 2, *ad* 1.
81. Thomas Aquinas, *Catena aulrea, in Ionnis Evangelium*, ch. 15, n. 4 (*ex Augustino).*
82. Bernard, *In Nativitate B. V. M., Sermo de aquaeductu*, n. 8, ML 183–442.

Chapter IX

1. Saint Teresa of Ávila, *Interior Castle: Sixth Mansions*, ch. 10; *The Life of the Holy Mother Teresa of Jesus*, ch. 18, 22, in *The Complete Works*, edited by E. Allison Peers (New York: Sheed and Ward, 1963).
2. Teresa of Ávila, *Life,* ch. 18, ch. 22.
3. *Vitae Patrum*, book 1: *Vita Sanctae Thaisis, meretricis* (author uncertain), ch. 2–3, ML 73–662.
4. Iuncta Bevegnas, *De vita et miraculis B. Margaritae de Cortona*, (Siena, 1897), ch. 4, n. 9; cf. Marchese, *Vita*, book 1, ch. 18, n. 5.
5. Teresa of Ávila, *The Way of Perfection,* ch. 18.
6. Ibid., ch. 15; Yepes, *Vita*, book 3, ch. 7–8.
7. Saint Bonaventure, *Legenda S. Francisci,* ch. 6, n. 6, *Opera*, vol. 8, (ad Claras Aquas, 1898), p. 521.
8. Vincenzo Puccini, *Vita* [of Saint Mary Magdalen de Pazzi] (Venice, 1611), part 5, *Seconda notte*, p. 387 and *Terza notte*, pp. 452–453.
9. Luigi Muños, *Vita* (Milan, 1667), book 3, ch. 23, pp. 403–404.
10. Thomas à Kempis, *The Imitation of Christ*, book 3, ch. 7.
11. Cited by Henry Suso, sermon 4 (Cologne, 1588), p. 217.
12. Puccini, *Vita*, (Florence, 1611), part 2, ch. 12.
13. Marco da S. Francesco, O. C., *Vita*, book 3, ch. 1, n. 10; *Opere del Santo* (Venice, 1747), vol. 3.
14. Saint Francis de Sales, Letter 2069 *(Fragments),* á la *Mère de Chantal* (1605–1609), *Oeuvres*, XXI.
15. Thomas à Kempis, *The Imitation of Christ*, book 3, ch. 46.
16. Saint John Chrysostom, *In Acta Apostolorum*, homily 6, n. 4, MG 60–62.
17. Thomas à Kempis, *The Imitation of Christ*, book 3, ch. 49.
18. Saint Jane de Chantal, *Entretiens faits à la récréation et aux assemblées de la Communauté*, XIX, *Vie et Oeuvres*, II, 284–285.
19. Saint Bernard, *In Cantica*, sermon 42, n. 3, ML 183–988, 989.
20. John Chrysostom, *In Matthaeum*, homily 68 (69), nn. 1–2, MG 58–639 to 642, MG 57–341 to 344.
21. Pietro Giacomo Bacci, *Vita*, book 2, ch. 17, n. 22.
22. Teresa of Ávila, *The Way of Perfection,* ch. 15.

Chapter X

1. Saint Hilarius, Commentarius in Matthaeum, ch. 3, n. 5, ML 9–930, 931.
2. Luke Wadding, *Annales Minorum*, for the year 1445, nn. 16–18.
3. Saint Teresa of Ávila, *The Way of Perfection*, ch. 36 in *The Complete Works*, edited by E. Allison Peers (New York: Sheed and Ward, 1963).
4. Saint Bonaventure, *Legenda S. Francisci*, ch. 6, n. 1.
5. Saint Augustine, *Contra litteras Petiliani Cenatistae*, book 3, ch. 7, n. 8, ML 43–352.
6. Teresa of Ávila, *The Way of Perfection*, ch. 15.
7. Jean Pierre Camus, *Esprit de S. François de Sales*, part 12, ch. 3.
8. Louis Abelly, *Vie* [of Saint Vincent de Paul], book 3, ch. 13, section 2.
9. Vincenzo Puccini, *Vita* [of Mary Magdalen de Pazzi], (Florence, 1611), part 4, ch. 31.
10. Teresa of Ávila, *The Way of Perfection*, ch. 7.
11. Puccini, *Vita*, (Venice, 1671), *Aggiunta*, at the end, *Dette e sentenze della Santa*, §5, n. 14.

Chapter XI

1. Pietro Giacomo Bacci, *Vita* [of Saint Philip Neri], book 2, ch. 15, n. 14.
2. Saint Teresa of Ávila, *Maxims for Her Nuns*, 36 in *The Complete Works*, edited by E. Allison Peers (New York: Sheed and Ward, 1963).
3. Cf. Saint Teresa of Ávila, *The Life of the Holy Mother Teresa of Jesus*, ch. 40.
4. Ibid., ch. 34.
5. Saint Augustine, *De consensu Evangelistarum*, book 1, ch. 12, n. 18, ML 34–1050; ch. 18, n. 26, ML 34–1053, 1054.
6. Saint Jerome, *Epistola 22* ad Eustochium, *De custodia virginitatis*, n. 25, ML 22–441.
7. Saint Jane Frances de Chantal, *Déposition pour la canonisation de S. François de Sales*, art. 26, *Vie et Oeuvres*, vol. 3.
8. Saint John of the Cross, *Ascent of Mount Carmel*, book 1, ch. 11.
9. Teresa of Ávila, *Carta* 421, *a la M. Ana de Jesús*, Priora de Granada, *y a sus religiosas*, May 30, 1582.
10. Vincenzo Puccini, *Vita* [of Mary Magdalen de Pazzi], (Venice, 1611), part 1, ch. 54.
11. John Cassian, *De coenobiorum institutis*, book 4, ch. 3–10, ML 49–154, 163.
12. Saint Gertrude, *Legatus divinae pietatis*, book 4, ch. 26.
13. Teresa of Ávila, *The Way of Perfection*, ch. 28.
14. Thomas à Kempis, *The Imitation of Christ*, book 3, ch. 37, n. 14.
15. Teresa of Ávila, *Life*, ch. 39.
16. L. da Ponte, *Sentimenti e lumi spirituali*, (Rome, 1690), §8, n. 33.
17. The source of this story is unknown.
18. Pontificale Romanum, *De benedictione et consecratione Virginum*.
19. Jean Pierre Camus, *Esprit de S. François de Sales*, part 3, ch. 27.
20. Galluzzi, S. J., *Vita*, book 4, ch. 1.

21. Petrus Blesensis, *Sermo* 46, *In festo Omnium Sanctorum* sextus, ML 207–699, 700.
22. Saint Francis de Sales, Letter 1966, (n.d.), *à la Mère de Chantal, Oeuvres*, (Annecy, 1908), XXI.
23. Teresa of Ávila, *The Conceptions of the Love of God,* ch. 6.
24. Saint Basil, *Regulae fusius disputatae, Opera* (Paris, 1637), II, p. 539, MG 31–925.
25. Saint Francis, *Oratio quotidiana B.P. Francisci*, in *Opera S. Francisci* (Pedeponti, 1739), book I, p. 20; Bartholomaeus de Pisis, *Liber conformitatium* (Milan, 1513), folio 41.
26. Thomas à Kempis, *The Imitation of Christ*, book 3, ch. 34, nn. 1–3.
27. Giussano, *Vita* [of Saint Charles Borromeo], book 8, ch. 11.
28. Patrignani, *Menologio di C. di G.*, May 24.
29. Saint Thomas Aquinas, *Summa Theologica*, II–II, ques. 189, art. 6.
30. Ibid, art. 10.
31. Saint Bernard, *Epistola* 111, *ex persona Eliae monachi ad parentes suos*, ML 182–255.
32. Lud. Habert, *Theologia dogmatica et moralis, De sacramento Ordinis*, part 3, ch. 1, §2.
33. Ibid.
34. Related by P. Rosignoli, S. J., *La saggia elezione,* part 1, ch. 2, §1, in *Opere* (Venice, 1713), III, 451.
35. Thomas Aquinas, *Contra pestiferam doctrinam retrahentium homines a religionis ingressu*, ch. 9, in *Opera* (Rome, 1570), vol. 17, folio 110.
36. Concilium Tridentinum, *Sessio* 23, *Decretum de reformatione,* ch. 11.
37. Thomas Aquinas, *Summa Theologica,* II–II, ques. 184, art. 8.
38. Ibid., ques. 189, art. 1, *ad.* 3.
39. Saint Alphonsus Liguori, *Moral Theology*, book 6, treatise 1, ch. 2, nn. 63–77.
40. Saint Anselm, in *Opera S. Anselmi* (Cologne, 1612). Ven. Herveus, *In Epistolam ad Hebraeos*, ch. 5, ML 181–1565.
41. Louis Abelly, *Sacerdos christianus, seu Manuductio ad vitam sacredotalem pie instituendam,* (Cologne, 1698), part 1, ch. 4.
42. Hor. Tursellinus, S. J., *Vita* [of Saint Francis Xavier], book 6, ch. 7; D. Bartoli, *Vita di S. Ignazio*, book 4, §12.
43. Saint Francis of Assisi, *Opusculum de vera et perfecta laetitia,* in *Opera* (Pedeponti, 1739), book 1, p. 16.
44. Bernard, *In tempore Resurrectionis*, *Sermo* 3, n. 3, ML 183–289, 290.
45. Bernard, *In Cantica*, *Sermo* 71, n. 14, ML 183–1128.
46. Bernard, *Sermones de diversis*, *Sermo* 26, n. 3, ML 183–611.
47. Puccini, *Vita*, (Venice, 1611), part 3, pp. 17–18.
48. Teresa of Ávila, *Interior Castle: Fifth Mansions*, ch. 1–2; *The Way of Perfection,* ch. 28.
49. C. Marabotti and E. Vernazza, *Vita* [of Saint Catherine of Genoa], ch. 29.
50. Saint John of the Cross, *Ascent of Mount Carmel*, book 1, ch. 13.

Chapter XII

1. L. da Ponte, *Vita* [of Baltasar Álvarez], ch. 40, §1.
2. Saint Teresa of Ávila, *The Spiritual Relations*, II and III, in *The Complete Works*, edited by E. Allison Peers (New York: Sheed and Ward, 1963).
3. *Acta authentica Canonizationis S. Teresiae*: auditorum rotae facta Paulo PP. V. *Relatio altera*, in *Acta Sanctorum* (Bollandists), October 15, n. 1233.
4. Saint Jane Frances de Chantal, *Déposition pour la béatification de S. François*, art. 37, *Vie et Oeuvres de la Sainte*, III, 185.
5. Saint Francis de Sales, *Introduction to the Devout Life*, part 3, ch. 2.
6. Jean Pierre Camus, *Esprit de S. François de Sales*, part 5, ch. 2.
7. Jane Frances de Chantal, *Déposition*, art. 37, *Vie et Oeuvres,* III, 185–186.
8. Saint John Chrysostom, *In Genesim*, homily 58, n. 5, MG 54–512.
9. Francis de Sales, Letter 290, *à Mère de Chantal*, *Oeuvres* (Annecy, 1823), XXI.
10. Saint Bernard, *De consideratione*, ad Eugenium PP., book 2, ch. 11, ML 182–755.
11. Andre Hamon, *Vie* [of Saint Francis de Sales], book 6, ch. 4.
12. Francis de Sales, Letter 502 (n.d.), *à la Baronne de Chantal*, *Oeuvres,* (Annecy, 1906), XXIV.
13. Camus, *Esprit*, part 16, ch. 9.
14. Francis de Sales, Letter 280, *à Madame Bourgeois*, April, 1605, *Oeuvres* (Annecy, 1904), XIII. See above, ch. 8, n. 2.

Chapter XIII

1. Blessed Henry Suso, *De Veritate dialogus, Appendix quarumdam sublimium quaestionum*, ch. 16, *Opera* (Cologne, 1588), p. 321.
2. Saint Augustine, *In Epist. Ioannis ad Parthos*, treatise 7, ch. 4, n. 8, ML 35–2033.
3. Saint Teresa of Ávila, *The Book of the Foundations,* ch. 5; *The Way of Perfection,* ch. 16 in *The Complete Works,* edited by E. Allison Peers (New York: Sheed and Ward, 1963).
4. Louis Abelly, *Vie* [of Saint Vincent de Paul], book 3, ch. 5.
5. Teresa of Ávila, *The Life of the Holy Mother Teresa of Jesus*, ch. 30, in *The Complete Works,* edited by E. Allison Peers (New York: Sheed and Ward, 1963).
6. Teresa of Ávila, *The Book of the Foundations,* ch. 5.
7. Teresa of Ávila, *The Interior Castle: Fifth Mansions*, ch. 3.
8. Saint Dorotheus, *Doctrina* VII, nn. 4, 6, MG 88–7102, 1706.
9. Saint Jane Frances de Chantal, *Entretiens faits à la récréation et aux assemblées de la Communauté, Entretiens*, 69, 73, and *Fragments d'entretiens*, *Vie et Oeuvres*, (Paris, 1875), II.
10. Abelly, *Vie*, book 3, ch. 21.
11. Teresa of Ávila, *The Book of the Foundations*, ch. 5.
12. Suso, *Opera* (Cologne, 1588), sermon 2, pp. 182ff.

13. Saint Francis de Sales, *Les vrais entretiens spirituels*, n. 2, *Oeuvres*, (Annecy, 1895), VI.
14. Thomas à Kempis, *The Imitation of Christ*, book 3, ch. 5, n. 32.
15. L. da Ponte, *Vita* [of Father Baltasar Álvarez], ch. 50, §1.
16. Teresa of Ávila, *Life*, ch. 10.
17. Blessed John of Ávila, *Lettere spirituali* (Rome, 1669), part 1, letter 41.
18. Vincenzo Puccini, *Vita* [of Saint Mary Magdalen de Pazzi], (Florence, 1611) part 1, ch. 59; *Detti e sentenze* (Venice, 1671), §5, nn. 33–34; *Vita* (Florence 1611), part 4, ch. 31.
19. Francis de Sales, Letter 282, around April 20, 1605, *â la Présidente Brûlart, Oeuvres* (Annecy, 1904), XIII.
20. Teresa of Ávila, *The Way of Perfection,* ch. 32.
21. Abelly, *Vie*, book 3, ch. 14.
22. Francis de Sales, *Les vrais Entretiens spirituels*, n. 14, *Oeuvres*, (Annecy, 1895), VI.
23. Francis de Sales, Letter 1290, *à la Mére Fave*, March or April, 1617, *Oeuvres*,(Annecy, 1895) XVIII, 359–61.
24. Teresa of Ávila, *The Book of the Foundations,* ch. 8, 24; *Life,* ch. 26; Yepes, *Vita*, book 2, ch. 27.
25. Teresa of Ávila, *The Book of the Foundations,* ch. 5.
26. Alonso Rodriquez, S. J., *Esercizio di perfezione*, part 3, treatise 5, ch. 7, n. 15.
27. Puccini, *Vita*, part I, ch. 61; part 4, ch. 30.
28. Saint Bridget of Sweden, *Revelationes S. Birgittae*, (Venice, 1671), book 4, ch. 26.
29. Jos. Juvencius, S. J., *Historia Societatis Jesu*, part 5, book 24, §46 (1605); cf. Patrignani, *Menologio*, May 23 (1605).
30. Puccini, *Vita,* (Venice, 1671) at the end, *Detti e sentenze della Santa*, §3, n. 21.
31. Pietro Giacomo Bacci, *Vita* [of Saint Philip Neri], book I, ch. 20, n. 23.
32. Ibid., n. 21.
33. Francis de Sales, *Introduction to the Devout Life*, part I, ch. 4; Blessed John of Ávila, *Trattato spirituale sopra il verso, "audi, filia,"* ch. 55.
34. Saint John of the Cross, *Ascent of Mount Carmel*, book 2, ch. 20 (also 22).
35. Gallizia, *Vita,* book 6, §21, *Massime che riguardano noi stessi*, n. 12, 27.
36. Salmanticensis Collegii Ord. Carm., Disc., *Cursus theologiia moralis,* treatise 20, ch. 7.

Chapter XIV

1. L. da Ponte, S. J., *Vita* [of Father Baltasar Álvarez], ch. 3, §2.
2. Louis Abelly, *Vie* [of Saint Vincent de Paul], book 3, ch. 23.
3. Ibid.
4. Saint Jane Frances de Chantal, *Déposition pour la Béatification et Canonisation de S. François de Sales,* (Procès d'Annecy, 1627), art. 31.

5. Saint Teresa of Ávila, *The Way of Perfection*, ch. 11, in *The Complete Works*, edited by E. Allison Peers (New York: Sheed and Ward, 1963).
6. Longaro degli Oddi, *Vita* [of Lu. da Ponte], book 2, ch. 1, nn. 13, 15.
7. Saint Bonaventure, *Legenda S. Francisci*, ch. 14, n. 2, *Opera* (ad Claras Aquas, 1898), vol. 8, p. 546.
8. Blessed John of Ávila, *Lettere spirituali*, part I, *A un sacerdote infermo* (Brescia, 1728), pp. 135–136.
9. See Saint Vincent de Paul, *Correspondence, Entretiens, Documents*, (Paris, 1920–25), VIII, p. 47.
10. Saint Francis de Sales, *Traité de l'amour de Dieu*, book 9, ch. 2.
11. Teresa of Ávila, *Mercedes de Dios*, XXXVI, *Obras*, (Burgos, 1917).
12. Teresa of Ávila, *The Way of Perfection*, ch. 15.
13. See the two biographies (*Vita prior et posterior*) in the Bollandists, *Acta Sanctorum*, April, 14.
14. Zaccaria Boverio, O. F. M. Cap., *Annali dell'Ordine dei FF. MM. Cappuccini*, for the year 1612.
15. Laurentius Surius, *De probatis sanctorum historiis*, March 29, *Martyrium SS. Jonae et Barachisii*.
16. L. da Ponte, *Vita* [of Father Baltasar Álvarez], ch. 18, §1.
17. Bollandists, *Vita posterior*, part 3, ch. 6, n. 224.
18. Simeone Metafraste.
19. Saint Basil, homily 18, *In Gordium martyrem*, n. 4, MG 31–499.
20. Saint Bernard, *In cantica*, *Sermo* 61, nn. 7–8, ML 183–1074.
21. V. Cepari, *Vita* [of Saint Aloysius Gonzaga], part 2, ch. 26.
22. Alonso Rodriguez, *Esercizio di perfezione*, part 1, treatise 8, ch. 20, n. 8.
23. Saint Augustine, *Soliloquiorum animae ad Deum liber unus*, in *Opera S. Augustini*, ML 40–865.
24. Augustine, *Sermo* 85 (*de tempore* 205), ch. 3, n. 3, ML 38–521.
25. Saint Francis of Assisi, *Opera S. Francisci*, (Pedeponti, 1739), vol. 1, p. 20.
26. Teresa of Ávila, *The Book of the Foundations*, ch. 14.
27. Elsewhere Saint Alphonsus attributes this statement to its true author, Saint Augustine. See *Sermo* 112, ch. 6, n. 6, ML 38–646.
28. Saint John Climacus, *Scala Paradisi*, Gradus 17.
29. Saint Laurence Gustiniani, *De disciplina et perfectione monasticae conversationis*, ch. 2, *Opera*, (Lyon, 1628), p. 82.
30. Saint Bernard, *In Cantica*, *Sermo* 21, n. 8.
31. Blessed Angela of Foligno, *Vita et opuscula*, book 2, part 2, *De libro vitae qui est Christus*, ch. 2.
32. Bollandists, *Acta Sanctorum*, April 26, n. 1.
33. Bernard, *Epistola* 100, ML 182–235.
34. Bernard, *De adventu Domini*, *Sermo* 4, n. 5., ML 183–49.
35. Francis de Sales, *Introduction to the Devout Life*, part 3, ch. 16.
36. Guiseppe Guarnieri, *Vita*, (Rome, 1689), book 2, ch. 9.
37. Giovanni de Palma, *Vita*, book 3, ch. 15.
38. Vincenzo Puccini, *Vita* [of Saint Mary Magdalen de Pazzi], (Florence, 1611), part 4, ch. 30.

39. Liero (Van Lyere), *S. Ignatii de Loyola Apophtegmata sacra*, (Antwerp, 1662), *Apoph.* 3.
40. V. Cepari, *Vita* [of Saint Aloysius Gonzaga], part 2, ch. 23.
41. Silos, *Historiarum Clericorum Regularium*, part 2 (Rome, 1666), book 4 (for the year 1606), p. 184.
42. Blessed Henry Suso, *Vita*, ch. 22.
43. Pietro Giacomo Bacci, *Vita* [of Saint Philip Neri], book 1, ch. 18.
44. Marco di S. Francesco, Carm. Sc., *Vita di S. Giovanni della Croce*, book 3, ch. 5, in *Opere del Santo* (Venice, 1747), vol. 3.
45. Teresa of Ávila, *The Way of Perfection,* ch. 13.
46. Thomas de Lentini, *Vita*, ch. 1, n. 6 in the Bollandists, *Acta Sanctorum*, April 29.
47. Luke Wadding, *Annales Minorum*, for the year 1319, n. 5.

Chapter XVI

1. Saint Thomas Aquinas, *Summa Theologica*, I–II, ques. 40, art. 7, c.
2. Louis Abelly, *Vie* [of Saint Vincent de Paul], book 3, ch. 3, §§1–2.
3. Thomas Aquinas, *Summa Theologica*, I–II, ques. 65, art. 5.
4. Saint Francis de Sales, *Traité de l'amour de Dieu*, book 10, ch. 10.
5. Thomas Aquinas, *III Sententiarium*, distinctio 29, ques. 1, art. 4.
6. Ibid., *distinctio* 26, A.
7. Dionysius Areopagita, *De divinis nominibus*, ch. 4, §§12, 15, MG 3–710, 714.
8. Saint Augustine, *De Trinitate*, book 8, ch. 10, n. 14, ML 42–960.
9. Thomas Aquinas, *De veritate*, ques. 23. art. 8, *ad* 2.
10. Thomas Aquinas, *Summa,* II–II, ques. 44, art. 6.
11. *The Little Flowers of Saint Francis*, "On the Most Holy Stigmata of Saint Francis," consideration 1.
12. Thomas Aquinas, *Summa*, II–II, ques. 24, art. 9.
13. Saint Robert Bellarmine, *De Purgatorio*, book 2, ch. 7.

Chapter XVII

1. Saint Bernard, *In Quadragesima*, *Sermo* 5, n. 3, ML 183–179.
2. Henricus Gran, *Magnum Speculum exemplorum* (1480), dist. 9, exemplum 201.
3. Saint Augustine, *Confessions*, book 8, ch. 11. n. 27, ML 32–761.
4. Cardinal Vincent Gotti, *Theologia Scholastico-dogmatica*, t. 2, tr. 6, 9, 2, §3, n. 30.
5. Saint James, *Epistola* 22, ad Eustochium, n. 6, ML 22–398.
6. Saint Francis de Sales, *Introduction to the Devout Life*, part 4, ch. 7.
7. *De vitis Patrum,* liber III, sive *Verba Seniorum,* n. 35, ML 73–761, 762.
8. Pietro Giacomo Bacci, *Vita* [of Saint Philip Neri], lib. 2, ch. 13, n. 16.
9. Saint Alphonsus Liguori, *Moral Theology*, Book VI, n. 476.
10. Saint Teresa of Ávila, *Mercedes de Dios*, XXVIII, *Obras*, (Burgos, 1915).
11. Mère de Chaugy, *Mémoires*, part 3, ch. 27: "*De ses tentations*," *Vie et Oeuvres de Sainte Chantal* (Paris, 1874), vol. 1.

12. Saint Bernard, *In Nativitate B.V.M., sermo de aquaeductu*, n. 8, ML 183–442.
13. Bernard, *In Vigilia Nativitatis Domini*, sermon 3, n. 10, ML 183–100.
14. Francis de Sales, *Introduction to the Devout Life*, part 4, ch. 13.
15. Louis Abelly, *Vie* [of Saint Vincent de Paul], book 3, ch. 24, section 1.
16. Marco di S. Francesco, *Vita*, book 2, ch. 4, *Opere* del Santo, (Venice, 1747), part 3.
17. Francis de Sales, *Traité de l'amour de Dieu*, book 9, ch. 2.
18. Saint John of the Cross, *Notte Oscura del Senso, Opere* (Milan, 1928), vol. 2.
19. Saint Teresa of Ávila, *The Life of the Holy Mother Teresa of Jesus*, ch. 30, in *The Complete Works*, edited by E. Allison Peers (New York: Sheed and Ward, 1963).
20. Saint John of the Cross, Letter 13, *alla Signora D. Giovanni di Pedrassa*, October 12, 1589, *Opere* (Venice, 1747), Part II.
21. Teresa of Ávila, *Life*, ch. 11.
22. Saint Francis de Sales, Letter 2092, *à la Mère de Chantal, Oeuvres*, (Annecy, 1923), XXI.
23. Saint Teresa of Ávila, *Exclamations of the Soul to God*, XVII.
24. Mère de Chaugy, *Mémoires*, part 3, ch. 27.
25. Ibid.
26. Ibid.
27. Ibid.
28. Ibid.
29. Ibid.
30. Ibid., ch. 16.
31. Ibid.
32. Ibid., ch. 26.
33. Ibid., ch. 27.
34. Ibid, ch. 25–29.
35. Ibid., ch. 26.
36. Saint Francis de Sales, Letter 947 (1612–14), *à la Mère de Chantal, Oeuvres*, (Annecy, 1910), XVI.
37. Mère de Chaugy, *Mémoires de la Mère de Chaugy*, part 3, ch. 26.
38. *In dedicatione ecclesiae*, hymnus in utrisque Vesperis.

Summary

1. Saint Bonaventure, *Legenda S. Francisci*, ch. 6, n. 1, *Opera*, (ad Clarus Aquas, 1898), vol. 8.
2. Pietro Giacomo Bacci, *Vita* [of Saint Philip Neri], book 2, ch. 8., n. 4.
3. Thomas à Kempis, *The Imitation of Christ*, book 3, ch. 37.
4. Saint Jane Frances de Chantal, *Vie et oeuvres, vol. 2, Fragments du petit livret*, n. 11.
5. Bacci, *Vita*, book 1, ch. 20, n. 21.

Other works by Alphonsus Liguori...

Selected Writings and Prayers of Saint Alphonsus

Adapted by: John Steingraeber

ISBN: 978-0-7648-0025-2

Through these excerpts of Saint Alphonsus' own writings, readers will learn the importance of prayer and the love of God in their lives.

The Glories of Mary

ISBN: 978-0-7648- 0664-3

The Glories of Mary, widely regarded as Saint Alphonsus Liguori's finest masterpiece, has for two and a half centuries stood as one of the Catholic Church's greatest expressions of devotion to the Blessed Virgin. This classic work combines numerous citations from the Fathers and Doctors of the Church with Saint Alphonsus' intense personal piety to produce a timeless treasury of teachings, prayers, and practices.

Visits to Jesus and Mary

Excerpted From Visits to the Most Blessed Sacrament and the Blessed Virgin Mary

ISBN: 978-0-7648-1443-3

This is an abridged version of the popular *Visits to the Most Blessed Sacrament and the Blessed Virgin Mary,* by St. Alphonsus Liguori. In this edition each entry has been condensed to make it suitable for shorter visits to the Blessed Sacrament.

Also available in Spanish:

Visitas a Jesús a María

ISBN: 978-0-7648-1521-8

CPSIA information can be obtained at www.ICGtesting.com
Printed in the USA
LVOW01s1732210515

439363LV00007B/7/P